THE WALL

A Day at the Vietnam Veterans Memorial

Peter Meyer and the editors of

Photographs by
Bill Eppridge • Frank Fournier • Lori Grinker
Charles Harbutt • Joe McNally • Christopher Morris

Text by
Naomi Cutner • David Ewing Duncan • Janet Mason
Sue Allison Massimiano • Sasha Nyary • Steven Petrow
Henry Sidel • Stephanie Slewka

TO THOSE WHO SURVIVED

A Thomas Dunne Book

Produced by Wieser & Wieser, Inc.
118 East 25th Street
New York, NY 10010

Designed by Tony Meisel

Printed in the United States of America.

ISBN 0-312-09478-7

First Edition
10 9 8 7 6 5 4 3 2 1

CONTENTS

FIELDER • JOHN M GLASSER • JOSEPH L MILLER • DOUGLAS R MOWBRAY • THOM
R SMALLIDGE • LLEWELLYN A SMITH • WALTER J SPAINHOUR Jr • JOSEPH H SULLIV
D WITCHER III • JAMES J ANGELIDES • JERRY W McCULLOUGH • JOE M BALLIN Jr
L BRACKETT • BENJAMIN A CHITKO • ALAN DANCE • GERALD W EVENHUS • HO
GAUSE • JAMES R GRIFFIN • THOMAS H HAWKING • BENJAMIN A KENISON • JO
W MOODY • LARRY J BAKER • DAVID L O'CONNOR • JOHN ONOFRE OQUENDO
D RAINWATER • EDWARD G RANKIN • JOHN L ROBERTSON • WILLIAM J ROHAN
D G StJOHN • RICHARD S BATES • NICHOLSON BROWN • DENNIS L BUNTING • L
G CUMMINGS Jr • JOHN R CUMMINS Jr • FRANK F DOUGLAS • DENNIS K EAKER
FERGUSON • GEORGE R FITZGERALD • WILLIAM G FLEMING Jr • GLENN E INSPRU
KIGER • BILLIE D LANDERS • HAROLD P LEAPHART • JOHN R LEE • DAREL D LEETU
LOCKWOOD • JOSEPH B MACK Jr • CHARLES E MacMICHAEL • EDWARD D McC
D McCRACKEN • ALFRED McPHERSON • MICHAEL C NATIONS • ALAN J O'BRIEN
D RAMOS • MICHAEL C REED • ROBERT E ROCKY • CLAIBORNE L SHAW • WILLIAM
M SMAY • CHARLES E STOKES • MICHAEL E SURWALD • ARTHUR WATSON Jr • DO
BAYNE • DAVID R BEATTIE • WILLIAM R HINERMAN • JOHN A BRYAN • ELMO ROSA
D GEOGHEGAN • HERSCHEL P HELM Jr • ELMER L BOATMAN • THOMAS C JONO
T F MURPHY • TIMOTHY J McMAHON • JAMES P NARD III • McARTHUR NICHOLS
H ROWLETT • DANNY RAY RUNDLE • FLORENTINO J SANTANA • PHILLIP E TAYLOR
B BACKEBERG • EARL J BAUCHMANN • JERRY L BRANSON • FRANK M BROWN Jr
M S DAVIS III • MICHAEL D DEROSIER • RONALD C DEXTER • JERRY W DOWNS • LA
E GLOVER Jr • WARREN L GOULD • GOLLIE LEO GRANT • JOHN M HARRINGTON
A HENRY • LINWOOD M HOLMES • CHESTER S HUGHES • ALBERT S HURTADO • C
RD F LANE • JOSE MARTINEZ-SOTO • GARY L MILLER • GEORGE W MILLER • JEROME
D L ENGLAND • JOSEPH D McNULTY • DON B PARSONS Jr • RICHARD W PERRY • T
T A POWELL • MATIAS T RODRIGUEZ • RONALD L TAYLOR • JI   WALDREP
EW W YOUNGKIN Jr • CHARLES J   M LOO   JAMES R BRANN
H EGGLESTON • LARRY GLOV   WAL   RIS   ELIAS RANGE
P KAMINSKY • JAMES F PANZA   JOHNSON
E ROSSER • BRYAN B STOCKW   BAUDER • GL
ARREY Jr • ARTHUR C ALTER   A FRIEL • CARLTO
C HINES • NORMAN L HOYT   VERNELL JENK
W JOLLEY Jr • THOMAS J KANE   EDWARD
L PETTIFORD • ANTHONY B P   RAEMDO
RD P BARTLE • DENNIS D BRA   JOSEPH N
AM J FISHER • RONALD A HEIN   CHARLES A
Y LEE LAKEY • FRANCISCO HER   AN J NAPIER

FOREWORD

Jan C. Scruggs

For many years I told newspaper editors about a story waiting to be written: the record of a routine 24-hour period at the Wall. I had envisioned shifts of reporters documenting the amazing interaction and communion between the living and the dead at that sacred place. Finally an editor from LIFE, whom I had never talked to, had a better idea—why not send reporters *and* America's top photographers to do the job?

The Wall, after all, is one of those few places that merit such extraordinary scrutiny. Is there a place quite like those two acres in Washington, D.C., where so many tears are shed? Certainly there are other places of reverence where the faithful gather. Other great monuments honor war dead, in Moscow, London and Paris.

But the Wall is profoundly different from the world's great cathedrals and monuments. Where else do pilgrims leave behind such powerful symbols of pain and history? A wedding ring, a pair of cowboy boots, a flag that once draped a soldier's coffin, a teddy bear. Items like these have been left at this mysterious memorial, designed by a descendent of Chinese immigrants, Maya Lin, when she was a 21-year-old student of architecture at Yale University.

The idea for the Memorial evolved from my experience as a teenage infantryman in Vietnam. In 1977 I studied the experiences of the survivors of the Nazi Holocaust and Hiroshima. Many of them felt guilty that they had been spared when other lives were lost. The same was true for many Vietnam veterans. I reasoned that if a memorial of names could be built, the veterans would have a place to confront and perhaps make peace with the ghosts of their past. Maybe such a memorial could even be part of some healing for an entire nation, a nation still painfully recovering from its most divisive experience since the Civil War.

I began the effort to create the Memorial in 1979. Prominent Americans supported the effort, ranging from antiwar activist and former Presidential candidate George McGovern to General William Westmoreland, former commander of U.S. forces in Vietnam.

In 1981 the winning design was announced. The entire effort was nearly destroyed by Texas billionaire Ross Perot and a small group of disgruntled veterans who were unable to understand the eloquent beauty of this structure. The opponents of the Wall used clever names to arouse the public against the design—the Black Hole of Calcutta, the Black Gash of Shame, an Open Urinal, a Tombstone, a Black, Flagless Pit.

But once the Wall was built, the controversy became a footnote, remembered mostly by college students studying art history.

On November 13, 1982, I was privileged to stand on a podium looking out over a crowd of 150,000 people. "Ladies and Gentlemen, the Memorial is now dedicated," I said. The crowd surged forward as if to claim the Memorial as its own. On that day America's Vietnam veterans were finally welcomed home. A nation once bitterly divided found itself united by a sea of names which has touched the hearts of visitors ever since. Most walls separate and divide. This one has given a generation of veterans their long-denied dignity and helped to heal a nation.

In November of 1992 the Tenth Anniversary of the Vietnam Veterans Memorial was celebrated. A year of activities on behalf of the Vietnam Veterans Memorial Fund took me around the country. I met many still in pain from Vietnam, ranging from a retired Admiral still grieving over the loss of his son to a student wounded at Kent State. I also met many veterans who are still gathering courage for a pilgrimage to their Mecca—the Wall.

There have been other books about the Memorial. Thankfully, *The Wall* goes beyond the mere selection of moving photographs. The 24-hour period that you will read about and see in this book captures the essence of the Wall through a poignant description of the wide array of feelings and emotions experienced there—ranging from sadness to joy.

After reading this you will understand with great certainty why a black granite structure in Washington, D.C., has become America's most visited and most loved memorial.

IN THE BEGINNING

Maya Ying Lin

It has meant a lot for me to have done something that can help so many. I feel I might be the author, but I would like to remain fairly silent. The Wall is designed for you, for everyone to come and bring their thoughts and emotions to the Wall. You make it come alive, and I want to thank all of you for your service to this country.

Speech at the Tenth Anniversary Commemoration Ceremony,
Vietnam Veterans Memorial, Washington, D.C.,
November 11, 1992.

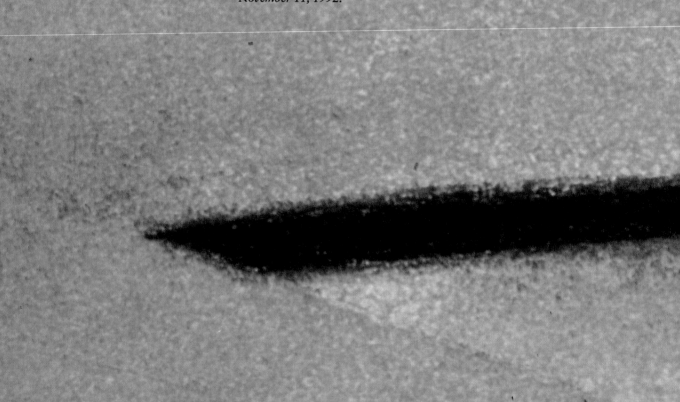

The designer's first sketch of the Wall

PREFACE: WAR AND MEMORY

I recall my Uncle Rene standing on a windswept hillside in Luxembourg, brushing tears from his eyes as he looked across a green field dotted with white crosses. "*Les pauvres jeunes hommes*," he kept repeating in his native French. "The poor young men." That field, with those crosses, was an unmistakable place. The simple similarity of the grave markers meant similarly violent deaths. In war. It was 1972, and my uncle, who had survived the German invasion and the fighting that raged through his front yard, was recalling 1942 as if the engines of destruction were then rumbling through the trees. His tears were real. His sadness. His pain. Thirty years had barely diminished the immediacy of the emotions.

The irony was that at that same time a parade of death out of Southeast Asia was leading another generation into a life of tearful memories.

How long it goes on. 1942. 1972. 1992. The scars of violence are difficult to erase. But they are more tender when sustained unnecessarily. Vietnam—a tiny country barely larger than Florida and Georgia combined—somehow stole our national innocence. From 1959 to 1975 American soldier boys were dribbled across the Pacific Ocean to fight and die in jungles and swamps while at home waves of their baby boomer brothers and sisters protested. An entire world watched. A generation's sensibility—of rebellion, cynicism, anger, loss of innocence, loss of confidence—was shaped by the 16-year conflict waged in the mud of Southeast Asia. It was less the humiliating defeat that caused this psychic shakedown than it was the length and vividness of the bloodletting, the gradual freezing up of the national will and conscience. Vietnam—the bodybags over there and the billyclubs here—remains for many Americans the air breathed in during three decades of national trauma and tragedy. Everything from the assassinations of Bobby Kennedy and Martin Luther King to the political scandals of Watergate and Iran-contra seem tainted by the original sins of My Lai and Cambodia. We can almost date the rout of national pride to the Tet offensive in January of 1968 or the Pentagon papers in June of 1971. We can trace our current civil wars to the rebellions at Kent State, Berkeley, even Watts. Guns and drugs seem as much the legacy of Vietnam as is Post Traumatic Stress Disorder. "The horror! The horror!" moaned Marlon Brando at the end of Francis Coppola's *Apocalypse Now*, summing up not just the war but also the national panic over the sudden loss of our way. A national PTSD. No more manifest destiny, perhaps no more destiny at all.

It was seven years after the last helicopter lifted off the roof of the American Embassy in Saigon before a memorial to the soldiers who died in Vietnam was built. Since there were no parades, it was too long to wait. But what could possibly memorialize the monumentality of the American defeat?

That was one question LIFE magazine wanted to answer when it sent a team of reporters and photographers to Washington, D.C., last August 4 to cover a typical day in the life of the Vietnam Veterans Memorial. The idea began as a suggestion from LIFE Director of Photography David Friend to commemorate the tenth anniversary of the Wall. And when photographer Charles Harbutt brought Friend a series of remarkable pictures he had taken of artifacts that had been left at the Wall over the years, we knew there was something there. Harbutt, who was a staff photographer for LIFE during the turbulent sixties, was well aware of the magazine's tradition: It had documented the war with a ferocity that earned its photographers and reporters many kudos and awards. (The only photograph in this book not about the Wall on August 4, 1992, is the picture by LIFE photographer Larry Burrows, one of the most heralded of war photographers, who was killed in Vietnam.) The pictures Harbutt showed LIFE were hauntingly simple. Soda cans. Medals of honor. Boots. Hats. Model cars. Love letters. It was enough to convince LIFE Managing Editor Jim Gaines to mark the anniversary. "There was something so poignant about the banality of these objects in contrast to the colossal scope of the war," recalls Gaines. "We had to try to document the interaction between the war and our national memory." The best way to do this, Gaines decided, was to document a typical day at the Vietnam Veterans Memorial.

On the afternoon of August 3, 1992, LIFE parked a rented RV under the trees of the visitors' parking lot near the west end of the Wall. It was sunny and hot. Except for the busload of veterans whom we knew would be visiting the Memorial that Tuesday, we chose the day at random. Melanie Griffith filming a movie that morning was a surprise; so was the news that the walkway in front of the Wall would be torn up for two months beginning August 5. And so too were people like

Virgie Hurst, a 76-year-old former draft board clerk from Aurora, Nebraska.

What was most remarkable about The Day was how poignant a backdrop the slick granite Wall was for recalling 20- and 30-year-old memories. "Facing The Wall," the resulting LIFE magazine cover story (November 1992), became a story about facing the war. The Wall, as one visitor describes it, is "a national Rorschach test." As Lisa Grunwald wrote in her powerful account of The Day, "The Vietnam War was a conflict in which it was never clear where the enemy was: a conflict without a reliable border, let alone a tangible wall. Ironically, the American monument to that war is a wall: The Wall. Fittingly, it is a wall that unites. Often it unites children with friends of their dead fathers. Sometimes it unites those who fought in the war with those who fought against it. Usually, because of the way its surface reflects the faces of onlookers, it unites the present with the past."

For 24 hours LIFE reporters and photographers, interns and editors, in shifts, watched and documented a remarkable procession. "I felt like I was back at the Grand Canyon, watching tourists joke and talk on their way to the Wall," remarked reporter Sasha Nyary. "But once they were in it, almost always, a hush came over them. They lowered their voices, slowed down, read the names. They realized it's a holy place, that, as one man described it to me, it's a cathedral."

When Assistant Editor Jan Mason arrived, she too was impressed by the silence of the crowd. "But more than anything else, it was the touching," she remarks. "Once, as I started up the west wall walkway, a Hispanic woman and her husband and teenage son asked a volunteer where panel 11W, Line 96, would be. And please could she have a paper to take a rubbing? The volunteer helped her find the panel and the number, and when she reached out to the name—Armando Cervera Luna—the woman cried out, 'There he is! There he is!' As she wept, she kept rubbing his name with her forefinger—as if trying to read it. As if it were Braille. So many people did that. Touch. You have to *touch* the Wall."

There was nothing easy about the reporting and photographing tasks that day: to intrude on the most public of private mournings; to capture, minute by minute, the grand diversity of the witnesses at the Wall; to stay out of one another's way. No one who worked on this story was unmoved; all were surprised by the power of the place.

"Though I worried about intruding into the private grief of these people," says Naomi Cutner, who spent twelve straight hours reporting, "I was repeatedly moved by how open they were about their pain and how willing people were to talk. A few couldn't. But for many the Wall seemed to give permission. For some it was even the first time they had told their story to anyone."

"A visitor can't see a name in the Wall without seeing her own image," remarked Stephanie Slewka. "She can't talk to a lost one without talking to herself. She can't escape being there."

Writer Sue Massimiano found the Wall "so confrontational that its silence speaks, and everyone feels impelled to answer. Who are you? Why are you here?"

It was the same question reporter David Duncan was asked by the Wall. "As I walk along the black slabs, surrounded by the dead, I find myself shedding my reporter's skin. I'm thinking about my five-year-old son and what it would mean to see his name here: SANFORD EWING DUNCAN. I look deep into the reflections on the polished black granite and imagine my boy staring back. I vow that I would rather die than see his name appear on this wall.

"I keep walking, scanning the names: Glenn W. Freeman, Daniel R. Fulwider, Enrique Lorenzo Garcia Jr. Like everyone who comes to the Wall, I touch one— James C. Hartney. Beside his name is a cross, an MIA. The stone is cold, the etched letters sharp.

"The names march on in neat, crisp, military order, like an endless tomb or a list in a bureaucrat's file. Yet there is no sense of officialdom here. The Wall is a sad and intimate place. You brush your fingertips across a name, and it briefly comes to life, the smooth surface reflecting back the color of your flesh. Each name has a story: the kid with the awkward grin who forgot to duck when the shrapnel flew; the girl left behind who married another man, one she didn't love, and comes back years later to lay a single rose against the Wall; the father who proudly watched his son go off to fight, only to spend the next few years in agony as the war unraveled and he realized his boy died for nothing.

"This is the power of this long black Wall: to tell stories; to elicit pain and grief; to offer a chance to remember and, hopefully, to heal. But remembering does not come easily to Americans. Maybe this is why the Wall is particularly painful for us, because it stands for something we want to forget, a horror planted amidst the easier memories of Washington—the soaring, white marble temples dedicated to oversized heroes. The names of the heroes on the Wall, by contrast, are only half-an-inch high."

This book grew out of a deep and abiding respect for those half-inch heroes. The testimony the LIFE team gathered during this one 24-hour period seemed too important a document not to present to the American public in a fuller form than was possible in a magazine story. All the reporters at the Wall filed moving accounts of their day; each photographer brought back hundreds of powerful pictures. The quantity and quality of their work made the task of creating a book relatively easy. Unfortunately it is not possible to give each contributor his or her due. They are a wonderful collaboration of talents.

And I speak for all the contributors when I say we hope that this book will become part of the history of the war, that it be a part of the revision of the American past that must inevitably continue. That this Wall offers us the place for such remembering and reshaping is a remarkable testament to its designer Maya Lin—and to those who gave their lives in the forlorn but innocent attempt to help others. But we also hope *The Wall* will be part of the fabric of this public communion with our fallen fellow citizens. We hope that in remembering them we will not forget how to live.

Peter Meyer
News Editor
New York City
February 15, 1993

1. BY DAWN'S EARLY LIGHT

August 4, 1992, 5:30 A.M. It is dark and quiet in Washington, D.C. Traffic signals along Constitution Avenue flicker from red to green above empty streets. Trees on the great grassy Mall stretch like dark waves from the lighted dome of Congress to the pearly light of the Lincoln Memorial. The 16th President casts his marble gaze eastward, toward the nearby shadows of a small grove of trees. There, a book the size of a Los Angeles telephone directory rests on a short, lighted pedestal, open to page 466. Like a phone book the page is lined with names, names from top to bottom. David John Moylan is one of them. Just one. One of dozens of names on the page; one of thousands of names in the book.

Thick glass, a few inches above the open pages, protects the book from the rain—but not from what are the obvious signs of eager, hesitant, curious, holy hands that have pawed the pages down to the nub of legibility. There are five books put out for visitors—each one replaced every other month. New books, same names. Same name, rank, date of birth, home state, date of death....frozen in death.

Between Gerald L. Aadlund of Sisseton, SD, who died May, 30, 1968, and David Lee Zywicke, of Manitowoc, WI, who died December 7, 1967, are 58,181 other names. None of them came back from a faraway place called Vietnam.

The glass is etched....

1959 IN HONOR OF THE MEN AND WOMEN OF THE ARMED FORCES OF THE U.S. WHO SERVED IN THE VIETNAM WAR 1975

It was the longest war in United States history.

The names ring with the diversity of the American population. Ames, Cole, Lizarraga, Gauthier, La Fleur, Demgen, Little Sun, Yamasaki, Lopez, Billie Joe Williams. There are two Billie Joe Williams.

But what were *they* doing in places like Bien Hoa, Pleiku, Hue, Khe Sanh, Quang Tri and Da Nang?

OUR NATION HONORS THE COURAGE, SACRIFICE AND DEVOTION TO DUTY AND COUNTRY OF ITS VIETNAM VETERANS. THIS MEMORIAL WAS BUILT WITH PRIVATE CONTRIBUTIONS FROM THE AMERICAN PEOPLE. NOVEMBER 11, 1982

The Memorial itself is a few dozen yards away: 58,183 names etched, half-inch high, on a chevron-shaped wall of polished granite that slices into the ground. You can hear your footsteps as you walk the stone pathway beside it, descending into the earth as if into a tomb. This is the Wall—America's open book of death. Dim spots along the path throw shards of light at the seemingly endless rows of names. Just names. A crow squawks. A jogger runs by, stops, gazes at the Wall. The crow squawks again. The names etched in the stone begin at the vertex of the V with the name of the first casualty, Dale R. Buis, in 1959, and run east "in the order taken from us." The list resumes at the low, west end of the Wall, and runs to 1975, where the last casualty, Richard Vande Geer, is listed, making the ten-foot high "fold" in the Wall the place where the killing begins and ends.

5:45 A.M. The sky begins to redden. The grass begins to turn from black to green. A few cars breeze along the broad avenues that cut through the trees. People are going to work. A woman carries a portable radio. Music. Get a whiff of cologne from a young man in a tight shirt. Another man stops by a vendor's stall selling Vietnam War t-shirts, already open at this early hour, and asks for a Boys' Large.

You can see the whole Wall now. There's Terry Lee Tebbetts. You can start to see the names. Ernest Lang. John Link. They are companions at the Wall. This is a cemetery. A mass grave. Though singly brave, they are not singly buried—nor forgotten.

STAGGS · JOHN J STAHL · JERRY W STANBERRY · EDWARD B STEELE
· THOMAS G STEVENSON Jr · HENRY R STROBO · WALTER STURGEON
UIST · RICHARD J SWEENEY · ERNEST W SWONER · MICHAEL J St ONGE
YNE TAYLOR · JERRY L TAYLOR · DAVID E THAXTON · FRED L THOMAS Jr
H TOBER · ROGER M TYNER · JAMES D TYUS Jr · BILLY L UNDERWOOD
N DANIKER · KENNETH E WADE · WOOTS E WADKINS · JOHN F WALKER
WASHINGTON · LESTER W WEBER · KELLY W WEITZEL · JAMES L WHITE
KINSON · WILLIE LEE WILLIAMS · CHARLES E WILSON · JOHN S WILSON
NICH · JOHN P ZIEGLER · JAMES C ALDERIDGE · XAVIER AMADO ARVIZU
ARBER · LARRY LEE BROOKS · THOMAS J BURGESON · MERLE F BUTLER
NTER · GILBERT M CHAVEZ · WILLIAM C CLINGER III · DANIEL COLEMAN
ROY H DAVIS · VASILIOS DEMETRIS · MICHAEL B DUFFY · JESSE R ELLISON
RUDITYS · LEWIS M FORMAN · THOMAS A GARMAN · HARLAN L HAH
MOTHY J HALL · E SCOTT HANCOCK · JOHN R HILL · MICHAEL N HUBER
SON · ADALBERTO R E VERDUGO · WILLIAM J LEVETT · HAROLD S LEW
W McALLISTER Jr · BYRON D McQUINN · JAMES NICKENS · JOHN C OD
N L POSPISIL · WILLIAM E PRICE · ALAN M ROYSTON · RICHARD W FOR
L SHIRODA Jr · RICHARD L SHUCK · GAROLD R SIMMERS · GARY W SMI
AYNE L THOMAS · RONALD T VARNEY · JOHN G JOYCE · JOSEP
CLARENCE J BABIN Jr · JEFFREY M BARRO
HAR

2. A PUBLIC GRIEVING

7:00 A.M. National Park Ranger Mike Lucas arrives at the War Memorial Information Booth, known as the rangers' kiosk, an hour early today. He has a couple of logistical problems—namely, Don Johnson and Melanie Griffith. Even though the Park Service has a special film department and even though thousands of movie and television crews have filmed or taped at the Wall since it was built in 1982, no one had told Lucas about this remake of *Born Yesterday*, and about superstars Griffith and Johnson—and the baggage: three big vans, dozens of men and women, actors, extras, technicians lugging cameras, tripods, chairs and lights—and a fully catered breakfast. Movie people. The day's first official visitors. Associate producers carrying coffee and walkie-talkies. Actors in military uniform; actors pushing strollers with plastic babies.

Lucas, who likes to run a tight ship, bustles about looking for the people with proper passes and clearances.

It is difficult to say whether Melanie Griffith's march along the Wall is fact or fiction. In her tacky halter top and short skirt she is strikingly beautiful—and very somber. Is she acting? Are the cameras rolling? The faces of the cast and crew are equally reverent, even off camera. Between takes, they stand and stare at the names on the Wall, reaching out to touch.... "I wore his POW bracelet for a year," explains a young associate producer, pressing her hand against a name.

8:00 A.M. An Eagle Management Recycling worker empties garbage bins into a truck at the curb above the reflecting pool. A nearby souvenir stand is empty; at another, t-shirts featuring a picture of a veteran at the Wall are already hung on lines for sale.

8:12 A.M. His patience gone, Mike Lucas closes the kiosk windows and dashes off to tell a location producer that the Wall is a public monument—not a movie set.

Lucas's colleague Donnie Smith isn't as upset about the film crew delaying its scheduled departure. The big NPS ranger from Texas got to be an extra. "They had me walk past Melanie Griffith about eight times," he says. "They didn't pay. Just walking past her was pay enough!"

There are no protests from the film crew as it packs up its gear. The extras file quietly on to the movie buses.

8:15 A.M. Ranger Lucas reopens the kiosk's windows, turns on the computer—which provides visitors with the location on the Wall of the names of loved ones and friends—and sets out his information brochures.

He says "Hi" to Julian Markham, a high school student who arrives as the day's first volunteer. Julian is one of 80 people who regularly donates time at the Wall. Known as "yellow caps"—for the color of the distinctive baseball hats provided by the nonprofit Vietnam Veterans Memorial Fund—they are a valuable help to the two or three NPS rangers who must monitor and help as many as 4,000 visitors to the Wall on any given day. "I've met people from different states. A lot of veterans. Mothers of people who are on the Wall, and fathers too," says Julian. "It's tough sometimes not to cry."

8:20 A.M. The morning life of the nation's capital is in high gear. Helicopters and planes are flying about—as they do all day in D.C. Buses disgorge commuters at the State Department complex across the street. A truck pulls up to a souvenir stall near the rangers' kiosk and a man unloads neck-to-waist mannekins—torsos that would soon wear Vietnam War t-shirts.

Music blares from a radio somewhere. More sweaty joggers run by on the perfectly green grass above the Wall. Helmeted bicyclists and a couple of roller skaters glide along a pathway toward the reflecting pool, luminous in the early sun, and whiz on to the Lincoln Memorial. NPS maintenance man Dewey Robinson has fired up a big mower and pushes it back and forth across the lawn above the Wall. The engine is loud and out of place on this quiet morning. Heat and humidity begin to drift in—with the tourists.

"Are all these people buried back there?" a young boy asks his mother.

Another boy says to his dad: "How long would it take to read all the names? I think it would take 50,000 hours."

How long would it take to live their lives?

8:25 A.M. Ranger Lucas is on his morning rounds—later than usual because of the movie crew. He first makes sure that the soldiers plaza is free of litter. An addition to the Memorial site in 1984—largely because Ross Perot, angry over Maya Lin's Wall design, lobbied for a second monument—Frederick Hart's seven-foot bronze sculpture, *The Three Servicemen*, stands on a small, landscaped plot a few dozen yards from the Wall. Lucas then checks that the trash cans are empty, that the chains around the lawn are intact, that the grass above the monument has been cut properly, "so nothing blows in the peoples' faces." He also checks that the soldiers' directories—on their glass-shielded podiums at the east and west entrances to the monument—are neat and ready for use.

At the kiosk again Lucas greets more of his unpaid help. "My faithful volunteers," he says with a broad smile. Emmelene Gura started volunteering more than eight years ago and has clocked 4,500 hours since then, the equivalent of two years worth of full-time work. Bobbie Keith, known as the "weather girl" in Vietnam for her broadcasts to the troops of weather conditions back home, has been at the Wall for two and a half years.

"I feel they gave their lives, I can give my time," says volunteer Gertrude Gerber who began in 1983, six months after the Wall was finished. "I wouldn't leave. It's so rewarding." Gerber is all business as she bustles around the kiosk, bussing Lucas, finding her soldiers' directory, her rubbing papers, her brochures. "The men and women who lost their lives got a bum rap and this Wall is helping to heal a nation," she says. "Families come. Vets come to look for their buddies. That's what really gets you. Tourists come. They're bewildered. In the time I've been here only one or two people didn't like the Wall. One wasn't sure he liked the design; the other said she didn't like it because it didn't have white marble and columns."

Mike Lucas stops to survey the Memorial grounds. Already a half dozen people are walking along the Wall. The air is warm, peaceful. "The first time I came, I knew I wanted to be here," says Lucas, a veteran of Vietnam who has worked at the Wall for five years. "This is my memorial. I take pride in it. I will stand in the sun, with the weather hot and humid, and I will have a good day. I'd rather be working at the Wall than anyplace else."

8:30 A.M. An older volunteer—a tall man with military bearing, wearing a short-sleeved yellow shirt with his yellow cap—stands quietly in front of a name on the Wall. He won't say who it is that he salutes. But he does it every time he comes. "There but for the grace of God—it could have been me," says Sidney George, one of the most loyal of Wall volunteers. Sid was in the Army in World War II, in Korea and in Vietnam. The 72-year-old retired Lt. Col. volunteers at the Wall because, as he says, "I feel fortunate to be here. I have dear friends and relatives named on the Wall."

Sid is an expert tour guide. "If you look past the names," he continues, "you also see life, you see your reflection and other people's reflections—all alive. The designer, Maya Lin, wanted us to see the past and the present simultaneously. That's why we have the reflective wall surface. And that's a healing idea too."

He works on Tuesdays and Thursdays and "whenever they call to say they need me." He's there on Memorial Day, the Fourth of July, Veterans Day and Christmas morning. "I come on Easter morning too," he says. "And I see some of the same people every Easter and Christmas. The same man comes every Christmas morning. We speak briefly each year. I myself started coming about six years ago. Yes, it was very difficult to come."

Sid knows the Wall as well as anyone. "There's Frank W. Jealous of Him—yes, that's his name, a Native American, and the W stands for Was. And this one too: Gabriel L. Two Eagle. Then over here it looks like a misprint. The same name inscribed twice. Billie Joe Williams and Billie Joe Williams. But it's no mistake. They were two different individuals, and they both died on 9 December, 1972," he says. "They came from adjacent states—Kansas and Missouri. One was a Marine; the other was in the Air Force. They join each other on the Wall."

Sid knows that the third Thursday of every month, men from the Veterans Affairs Hospital in Roanoke, Virginia, come to the Wall. "They come very early. It's part of the healing process for them."

"There are eight women's names on the Wall," he says. "Mary Klinker of the Air Force, from Lafayette, Indiana, and seven Army nurses." Sid extends his pointer and scribes the names at panel 5E: Carol A.E. Drazba, Elizabeth A. Jones. "They died on the same medivac flight on 18 February '66," says Sid, who still speaks the crisp argot of the military, adding weight to his words. "Because the names are arranged by date of death, every time you see the alphabet change, you know it's the start of a new day. There are 58,183 names on the Wall—all but these eight are men."

Most of the names have a diamond beside them, Sid explains, indicating that the death is confirmed. But there are still more than 1,100 names marked with a

cross—missing in action. Twenty-five years and still missing. When a death is confirmed, a diamond is etched around the cross—there are now 150 crosses within diamonds. And if ever someone were to return home alive, a circle would be etched around the cross. In the years after the Wall was built, as veterans have died from war-related injuries, almost 250 names have been added to the Memorial.

"The Vietnam War was sixteen years of conflict," says Sid. "During that time we had 58,183 casualties—dead and missing in action. In Korea, in 36 months, we had over 53,000; in four years of World War II, we had 405,000; and in World War I, in two years, 120,000. That's over 600,000 dead. The Civil War had 622,000. That's over a million in a little over 100 years. And what does that tell us? It tells us we're slow learners."

8:35 A.M. Earl and Beverly Dobrinska from Milwaukee, Wisconsin, search through the soldiers' directory for the name of their cousin's son, Tommy Dobrinska, a Marine. "It shouldn't a had to be," says Earl, a veteran of WW II.

National Park Ranger Helen Siskavich Hossley asks if she can help locate the name on the Wall. They nod. Dobrinska is 38 East, Line 67. She points toward a spot to the right of the fold. "It is the 38th panel to the right, sixty-seventh line from the top."

When Siskavich Hossley first started working here in March of 1991, she looked for the name of her kindergarten teacher's son, Michael Petrashune. "I was in the third grade then and he was nineteen. I remember how upset his mother was. It was a small town of just 1,200 people."

Siskavich Hossley watches the Dobrinskas walk off. "I used to be here at night," she says. "I liked it. All the monuments are lighted and it's quiet and there are not so many tour groups as during the day. And many vets need the cover of twilight or darkness to cope with their reactions to the Wall."

8:38 A.M. "I have been trying for ten years to come to this Wall," says Nick Gonzalez as he walked with his wife, Sylvia, by the soldiers statue. Both are wearing Marine Corps t-shirts.

"Until now, I don't think I could have coped with it emotionally," he says. "I probably would have broke down and made a fool of myself." Gonzalez suffered Post Traumatic Stress Disorder after his tour in Vietnam and spent five years trying to recover. He has flown from Texas just to see the Wall. "This visit is my final healing," he says. "I've been out now twenty-five years, and it's time to do it. This is the last hurdle for me. It still hurts, it's still there."

8:45 A.M. "My brother died in 1967, on Mother's Day," says Alan Broquist. Alan is standing in front of panel 19E with his two children and wife Anita, whose brother was also killed in Vietnam. "He is buried at Camp Butler in Springfield, Illinois," she says. "He was twenty-two. I was sixteen. He won a Silver Star for rescuing some of his buddies. He was doing what he shouldn't have been: being a hero. It was hard on my parents."

8:46 A.M. The parade of people along the stone pathway is now constant. And almost everyone touches the Wall at some point; children almost immediately, older people more slowly. Veterans and those with family or close friends named on the Wall walk very slowly, searching out a particular name. The sightseeing crowd is quicker, but nevertheless reverent, serious and respectful.

A Danish Marine says: "I came because everyone in Europe talks about this Wall."

Rosemary Duke, an Englishwoman on holiday, was a student demonstrator during the Vietnam War. "We were politically divided in Britain as in the States. At the time, I wondered what it was in South Vietnam worth defending. The government was deplorable. It's like Kuwait with Desert Storm. But I find the Wall very moving. One feels a sense of such waste. What did they die for?"

8:50 A.M. "When I first got back, the first five years, it was real rough," says Nick Gonzalez as he waits at the Wall while a volunteer searches the directory for the name of Nick's friend. "I would wake up at night screaming. I would kneel beside the bed shouting, 'Get down, they're coming.' I lost so many friends over there, I just don't think I could have coped with it before now."

Nick's wife adds: "One night, I found him curled up in the closet, giving out commands. He whispered them: 'You go over there, you over here.' It was really scary. But I didn't give up."

"The first guy killed was a Hispanic from California," says Nick. "His name was Hernandez. I can't remember the rest of his name, but I would like to find him today. When I first got to Vietnam, we got bombed real bad. A lot of guys were wounded. Hernandez and a few others were dead. I hated those mortars, falling day after day. You don't know where it's gonna land. You feel like, hey, I'm here today, and I hope I'll be here tomorrow. But you never saw the enemy coming. They slept with you, they ate with you, they hit you at night. It was hard to get any sleep, because you didn't even know if you were gonna wake up. It was hell, real hell.

"Another guy I knew up here somewhere on the Wall was this black guy, Dwayne Thomas. One time we were putting in extra concertina wire around the perimeter of headquarters in Da Nang. And there was a little village nearby—close enough so they could see that we did this

every day, same time. So, one morning the company lieutenant told me to go work someplace else, filling sandbags. I did. Then I heard a big booooom! Smoke and everything. They had booby trapped that wire, and my buddies had stepped on it. Two got killed; one of 'em was Dwayne. It could have been me. I was eighteen, and I kind of went out of my head. It hurt real bad."

8:55 A.M. Betsy Gochnauer from Walnut Creek, California, reaches up to help a short lady make a rubbing on the Wall. She doesn't know the woman or the name; it was simply a case of her being tall and the other lady short. "While I was reaching up, my arm began to quiver and shake," says Betsy. "It was a long reach. And it hurt. But I thought then of the sacrifice those people made—and my arm was fine." Shirley Pepper, from Georgetown, Delaware, was happy for the help. The name rubbed was Robert T. Anderson on panel E37, line 3. Killed in 1966. "We called him 'Sparky' in high school," says Shirley.

8:58 A.M. A lone Park Service worker empties the refuse containers near the vendors' stalls. James Hudson had been in Vietnam, at Bien Hoa and Long Binh. He was in

Cambodia too. "I have a couple of Purple Hearts somewhere at home," he says. "But I get a cold chill looking at the names of all the guys who died. I found one guy I knew—John Sprinkle from New York ; he died in 1970. I found him there." He nods in the direction of the Wall, then moves to the next trash bin.

9:00 A.M. Word spreads among the Park rangers that Senator Al Gore, the new Democratic vice-presidential candidate, may come by the Wall this afternoon. The

rangers have tried to dissuade his press people from having him do so. It would backfire on the Senator, they say, because people consider the Wall a sacred place—outside the bounds of politicking. [He doesn't show.]

The mood is subdued. There is crying, some weeping. After touching the Wall, a woman gasps.

Raymond and Jane Fertig say that they have wanted to come here ever since seeing The Moving Wall in their hometown of Ellinwood, Kansas, last fall. The creation of Vietnam veteran John Devitt, the Moving Wall is a 250-foot long, half-scale replica—made of 75 aluminum and plexiglass panels—of the granite memorial Maya Lin designed. Since 1984 Devitt has been traveling the country with his portable Wall, giving those who can't come to Washington a chance to honor the war dead. In Ellinwood it was seen by 15,000 people in just one week, say the Fertigs, and there was even a ceremony for Mark Holtom, the one person killed in the war known to be from their town. "Full size," they agree, "the Wall is much more impressive."

Cindy Kindig, from San Diego, is here with her two daughters, Cori, 10, and Sara, 8. "My dad was in Vietnam back in '70, my senior year," Cindy explains. "He's 65 now. It was hard. To me he was defending our country. It was easy for those against the war to say, `I don't believe in war.' That wasn't their dad over there."

Says Sara: "It's hard to believe all these people died in the war."

9:06 A.M. Along the west side of the Wall Allie Prescott, 44, and C.B. Baker, 46, look for Martin Schiller, a Sigma Alpha Epsilon brother from Memphis State University and a former Tennessee state champion in the 440-yard dash.

"Schiller went to Vietnam because of a woman," says Baker. "He had a fight with his girlfriend. I can remember him beating his fist on a brick wall. He was really shaken up."

"He was in the reserves with me," says Prescott, "on an educational deferment—the Dan Quayle rap. But after he broke up with his girlfriend, he wanted to go on active duty. So he went to Fort Bragg and got into this Green Beret stuff. He was killed on the second day over there. And then here he is on the Wall. And that's all you get for dying."

"Somehow it doesn't seem like enough," says Baker.

"I can see Schiller right now," adds Prescott, "I see him

running track. An eighteen-year-old kid, blond hair, a good-looking guy. I don't see him at all in military attire. I see him in shorts and a t-shirt, running. That's what he loved to do. I got a picture of him winning a race, breaking the string. That's how I remember him."

9:10 A.M. Nick Gonzalez is back at the kiosk for more help finding his buddy Hernandez. Like many vets who come to the Memorial, his information about his dead friend is sketchy. Nick remembers only a last name (Hernandez), a home state (California), a branch of service (Marine Corps) and the approximate time of death (January, 1965). Lucas puts the computer's database to work, but cannot find a "Hernandez" that fits Nick's description.

"Sometimes," he says, "looking for these guys is like a treasure hunt, with only half a map." Lucas suggests to Nick that he return to the Wall, to the panel corresponding to the date when his friend was killed. "If that's January, 1965," says the ranger, "he should be listed on panel 1 East, about line 81 from the top." Armed with this new information, a determined Nick Gonzalez marches back to the Wall. His hands shake as he searches panel 1E, counting down from line 81. He is so nervous that he seeks out another volunteer for help. Together they crouch and pour over the names on the granite with their fingers.

Suddenly, Nick stops, his finger on a name just a few inches above the ground. "That's it. That's him. *Fernandez*. Not Hernandez. Robert Fernandez. Is he from California?"

The volunteer looks up the name and reads: "Fernandez, Robert Sanchez, Private First Class. D.O.B. 4 May, '44. KIA, 20 May, '65. Stockton, California."

Nick leans close to the name of his friend, killed 27 years before. He whispers something. He slowly touches the name, his eyes moistening. Then this stony faced ex-Marine smiles softly.

"He was real quiet, like me," says Nick. "No drinking, or anything. We went to boot camp together. We used to talk a lot, in Spanish, about what we'd do when we got back home, girls, that sort of thing. And he didn't come back, and I did. I wonder all the time: Why was it him, why wasn't it me? Man, I just don't get it."

For a long time he stares at the name on the Wall.

9:11 A.M. John Coyne is pointing out the name of Michael R. Kempel, panel 7 West, to his young sons. "A high school friend," says Coyne.

But for him the Wall is as much about his Vietnamese wife, who refused to visit the Wall during this vacation trip, as his friend. In 1977 she and two siblings were sent to the U.S. by her father, who had been a successful hotel and restaurant owner in Saigon until the Communists confiscated the family's property. Two years later the remaining members of the family—parents, grandparents, aunts, cousins—all died while trying to escape on a boat filled with fleeing refugees. "My wife is bitter about the war," he says. "Her family lost everything. Then she lost her parents and many members of her family."

9:20 A.M. Nick Gonzalez and his wife are finally leaving. "This is good," he says, looking relieved, even happy, as if a weight has been lifted from him. "It's not my last trip to the long black Wall."

visited the Wall several times—and marching into the crease is a chore each time. This time, afraid he might lose control, he called his wife from a public phone near the Wall to ask her if she thought he could make it. She encouraged him to do so.

"There are over 100,000 homeless Vietnam vets. And most of them still suffer from PTSD. My first marriage fell apart. I was into alcohol and prescription drugs from the VA hospital." There were major differences between Vietnam and earlier wars, Engelbrecht says. "Men were taken in at age twenty-six in World War II, on average. It was age twenty-five for Korea. But it was nineteen for Vietnam. Men fought an average of thirty days at a stretch in World War II; in Vietnam, we averaged 300 days without a break because there was no safe spot behind the lines. In 'Nam the only territory a fighter owned was what he stood on. You were *always* in a fire zone."

Engelbrecht has founded the Real World Foundation to provide shelter and food to vets who need it. "Look, you take an eighteen-year-old away from his family, train him to kill, and within days or weeks he does kill and kill often. And what do you expect?"

He marched slowly into the crease and made a rubbing of a name. "I must know 125 guys whose names are on that wall," he says. "But I knew them all by nick-names—not last names."

9:30 A.M. It's getting hot and humid, and more people continue to arrive. A trim woman with a creamy complexion is leaning against the heavy chain railing, her hand on her mouth, staring at panel 9E with tears in her eyes. "It's been a long time," she says, "but that doesn't make it easier." Reneé Sulpizio, 44, is talking about her first husband, Robert Stallings, who died in Vietnam in July, 1966, age 18. "We had been married seven months, and he had been in Vietnam for two months when he was killed. It was just about twenty-six years ago to the day." Reneé had a son by Stallings—who had only seen pictures of his child—who is now 26. "I needed to be here now," she says.

In his letters to her, Stallings was lonely, she remembers, scared. But he enlisted in the Marines and though he didn't want to go to Vietnam, he knew he might, and he thought it was right to go. "He didn't understand the killing," she says, "but it was a case of you kill them or they kill you. He believed in the war, in the American dream of freedom. He was a patriot."

After he was killed, "I had a real rough time," she says. "I was so young." She remarried quickly, at 19, but it

9:21 A.M. Tim Bjorge, a high school teacher from Pipestone, Minnesota, is gazing at the smooth black granite. "The number of names is overwhelming," he says. Bjorge, on a sightseeing trip to Washington, doesn't know anyone who died in Vietnam; he has an uncle who fought and survived. "It's awesome to wonder, 'What did all these people die for?' And that's the bottom line. We ask ourselves why things happen, and it's tough to find an answer in this case."

9:22 A.M. Vietnam veteran Charles Engelbrecht, Bravo Company, 1st Battalion, 4th Marine Regiment, 3rd Marine Division—a native of Dale, Indiana. He was in Vietnam from November of 1967 to April of 1969, and now stands at the top of the pathway leading to the Wall.

"I am afraid I might flip out," he says. Engelbrecht has

didn't last. "It was a case of being so devastated and in shock," she says. "What saved me was my son. I knew I had to be strong and take care of him. He looks just like his father, and now he has a son. It was real hard for him not to know his father. He felt cheated. We both did."

9:31 A.M. The sidewalk along the Wall is thick with people. Tour groups arrive one after another. The tourists follow their "umbrella ladies," as the rangers call the tour guides, for the ubiquitous raised umbrellas they carry as locators for their charges. After ten years the Vietnam Veterans Memorial has become the most popular monument in all of Washington. More people visit the Wall in a year—over a million—than visit the Washington Monument or the White House or the Lincoln Memorial. The most unpopular war has produced the most popular monument....

9:45 A.M. Linda Graham rushes up to the information kiosk four minutes before her bus leaves and asks, "Who from Kokomo, Indiana, died?" She knows that two classmates died, but doesn't know which ones. "You hear about it, and then you finally get to the Wall, and it's, 'Yeah, they really did die.'" Mike Lucas prints out a list. Twenty-three names are on it. Population of Kokomo, says Linda, is about 45,000. She dashes for her bus.

9:58 A.M. A pale man in a wheelchair, accompanied by family members, rolls down the cobbled path. As he passes the names, he begins to cry. Stopping at panel E1, he looks at lines 84-86 and breaks down and sobs. Jim Hamilton was an Army E6, a helicopter mechanic, in the 119th Aviation Unit. He was in Vietnam for one combat tour, 1964-1965, having dropped out of high school to enlist at age 17. On February 7, 1965, he was sleeping when the Viet Cong overran his camp at Pleiku Air Base, the first all-American base attacked in Vietnam. Eight men in Jim's unit were killed. (The attack triggered the massive American bombing of North Vietnam, begun within hours of the Pleiku attack.) Now ill with diabetes and confined to his wheelchair, Jim says he wanted to see the Wall before he died.

"They hit us on the seventh of February, 1965. I will never forget that date. They come right over the top of us early in the morning. They mortared us. They strafed us. They just blowed us off the face of the earth. We were sleeping. I took some shrapnel." He looks at the names on the Wall. "There they are, there are their names. Alvin Parker. Theodore Lamb. Jesse Pyle." He starts sobbing again. "My best friend was Alvin Parker. He was my roommate. We always watched out for each other. When I see his name up there, I see his face. He was about 5'8", 5'9". He was a colored boy, a black boy. He'd give you the shirt off his back. He was on guard duty that night when they got him. I'll never forget him. I'll never forget him." More sobbing. "It was all such a waste, such a waste. One of the guys that got hit, it should have been me, he took it for me. Where's his name? Where's his name?" More sobbing. "We had the capability to win that war, and make these deaths mean something. But they wouldn't let us. I've been wanting to come here for ten years, but I haven't been able to, because of the pain. Now I'm real sick. If I didn't come now, I might not have made it. As I was comin' down here, I was lookin' forward to it, and scared, too. It's just unreal, unreal. I think this wall is the best, better than anything I ever dreamed of."

Before Hamilton leaves, he asks a volunteer to rub the names of the eight men.

Joseph Kenneth Belanger, age 20, Bingham, ME
Ralph Wayne Broughman, age 26, Covington, VA
David Craig, III, age 25, Pitcairn, PA
Gerald Dean Founds, age 35, Frankfort, KS
Theodore Lamb, age 25, Dundee, FL
George Markos, age 25, Ft. Worth, TX
Alvin G. Parker, age 24, Nashville, TN
Jesse Andrew Pyle, age 35, Springfield, OR

Hamilton holds the names up to his chest, his eyes closed, his grief overwhelming.

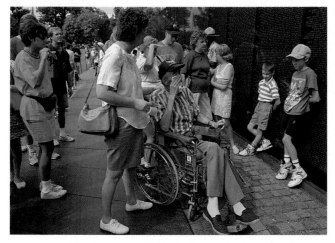

3. THE PARADE OF TOURISTS

10:00 A.M. "We had to see this," says a Dutch tourist, surveying the Wall from the sharp crease of the vertex. "You can see old buildings all over Europe, but this is really American. Unfortunately, too many were lost. They didn't accomplish anything with this war."

10:05 A.M. A man approaches the ranger kiosk. "Which way to the Kennedy Center?" he asks.

10:10 A.M. Mike Lucas gets his rubbing papers, pencils, directory and stepladder ready to go to the Wall. "Rain or shine or snow, I'm at the Wall," he says. He'll work the Wall some part of every day, talking to people, helping them find names. But most of his time is spent at the information booth, looking up names and statistics in the computer, giving directions, answering the phone. (The number is 202-634-1568.) "Vietnam Memorial. Mr. Lucas speaking," he says into the old, rotary phone. People call long distance. Television stations call. "How tall is the Wall?" they ask. "Ten feet in the middle," he says. Lucas keeps a book at the kiosk in case rain keeps visitors from getting rubbings. They write in their addresses and when the Wall is dry, a ranger or volunteer will do the rubbing and mail it to them.

10:15 A.M. Ken Marino, a former Marine from Virginia comes to the Wall often. "Too many names," he says sternly. In 1975, during the evacuation of Saigon, Marino was stationed off the coast of Vietnam. He had friends, neighbors and relatives who were killed in the war. He thinks the Wall—the "blackness" of it—works as a memorial. "It stares you back in the face," he says. "You see yourself in there. It could have been any of us."

10:25 A.M. A group from American Tour International, led by blonde-coiffed Honey Mahaffee, bearing an umbrella, breezes by Lucas. The ranger says hello and hands over a pile of brochures. "Danke schön," she says brightly.

"Do you have any in French?" a tour member asks.

Lucas smiles, but shakes his head no.

10:30 A.M. The walkway is thick with people moving steadily and quietly under the hot sun. Frank and Shaina Toppo, from Irvine, California, look through the soldiers' directory for a buddy of his. Fernando Loranzo. "We called him Cool Willie," says Frank. "I got out on the day of the Tet offensive and went to medical school on the G.I. Bill. He re-enlisted, for two more years. Not a good idea."

10:34 A.M. Mike and Kathy Dryer and their daughter Stephanie have come to Washington from Indianapolis on vacation. Mike probably would have gone to Vietnam, but he left the Air Force in May of 1965, just a few months before the big build-up. "I knew one guy who was wounded over there and never got right after that," he says. "He tried to kill himself. There's just no logic to the war. Why didn't we go in and really clean up? We didn't want to end it, we only had a commitment to being there."

10:45 A.M. Standing at the middle of the Wall, Heidi Randall, tall, blonde and 17 says, "I think the war was a shame and I don't think the Wall is enough." Heidi was born "the year it ended [1975]. I read a lot about it. My dad was very angered about the war. So I grew up hearing a lot about it." She's here to look for the name of Robert J. Randall Jr., her grandfather's brother. "My best friend and I studied up on it," she says of the war. "Coming here is like going to a cemetery. All these people could be alive."

10:55 A.M. Yellow cap Emmelene Gura perches on top of a stepladder in front of panel 15W, taking a rubbing of the name Freddie Long. Freddie's brother Benjamin stands at the bottom of the ladder with his wife and two children.

"Freddie was killed on a dozer, laying a convoy," says Ben, who had been in Vietnam before his brother. "They said a fifty-pound claymore blew him off of it." This is the first time Ben has been to the Wall. His eyes fill with tears as he remembers. "He had twenty-eight days left to go. He didn't even have to go out in the field, from what I understand, to run a convoy."

So he's a hero?

"He's dead," Ben says. "The heroes are the ones who refused to fight." He speaks quietly, in an emotionless

FRED M BAILEY

OHN E BRAID · JAMES J HO

· RICHARD C DANIELS

· EDWARD B FULGHAM

ODORE M HATLE · GARY E

· MONTE R

· CHARLES E KUHN

EORGE D McCLELLAND · BI

CHAEL E BARROW
STETTER • MARVIN M BU
ORGE D DEITRICK • DEW
ANSON T GERONZIN Jr •
NNER • TERRY A HOUSEHO
NES • PAUL D JONES • JEAN
DONALD T LASKAY • MARZ
W McDONALD • DANIEL R N

In you, O Lord, my refuge I take,
I will not be afraid.

monotone that barely conceals an intense anger.

"It's like the Gulf War. The President gets his tit in a wringer, we go kill some boys. If it would solve anything, I'd go do it tomorrow. But I don't want to be caught in a political campaign. I don't think anybody else does.

"I've studied since my brother got killed, and the biggest part I've found out about it is that it could have been prevented. Politicians start the wars and then they get the generals to run it. As soon as the generals get it in hand, the politicians take it back over....

"I thought I was protecting my flag and doing what should be done. But I realize now if I'd had more knowledge about what I was doing, I might have been standing up here on one of these steps, telling them to take me to jail. That's why they pick young and dumb 18-year-olds to fight. They don't want somebody that's had time to go think about it.

"The next war the politicians ought to go first. I'll go behind them. *Then* we'll send the young kids."

Ben looks at his kids. "If I can teach these children to think for themselves and not accept somebody else's thinking," he says, "if they'll do that, hopefully we won't have another Wall facing us this way, another one boxing us in. No more names. Because you don't ever get over it, you don't ever forget it. There's nothing you can ever do to change it. So what you have to do is change it before it starts."

11:00 A.M. Brad Ballinger, 17, from Sacramento, is here because "it's the thing to see." He found two Ballingers in the soldiers' directory and took rubbings of their names because "it might be family."

His girlfriend, Shannon Callahan, 16, also from Sacramento, points and says, "It could be any of us there."

To the west of the monument several veterans groups have set up booths in spaces reserved for demonstrators. Mostly men, mostly wearing military campaign caps, fatigues and combat boots—not unlike the clothes worn by many visitors to the Wall—they sell t-shirts and pass out literature promoting various causes.

Jerry Cunningham, 52, in the Navy for 22 years as an aviation electrician, wears fatigues and a floppy Desert Storm hat. His group, Americans for Freedom, Always!, only has "ten to fifteen members," he says. "But we sponsor parades and lectures, and lobby Congress on MIA issues. There are Americans we know who were

prisoners and who just disappeared. Where did they go?" The group raises much of its money selling t-shirts at the Wall (for $12) that proclaim "Saigon Lives in the Hearts of Those That Served" on the front and "Ours was a Noble Cause" on the back. The rest comes from members' own pockets. The group spent $30,000 on a float that traveled Pennsylvania Avenue in the "Rolling Thunder" parade welcoming home vets from Desert Storm.

"When I first heard about the Wall and heard they were going to put up black granite slabs and a hole in the ground, I said, `It figures,'" says Cunningham. "But it surprised me. It's one of the finest memorials I've ever seen."

Cunningham hands out a brochure: HOW CAN WE IN

THIS "LAND OF THE FREE" SIMPLY ABANDON OUR DEFENDERS? DOES OUR GOVERNMENT MAKE A MOCKERY OF OUR CREED "LIBERTY FOR ALL" BY ABANDONING OUR MIA'S TO AN EXISTENCE OF SERVITUDE IN ENEMY HANDS?

11:02 A.M. Patrick Wemple, from North Carolina, is visiting the Wall for the second time. His father is there, killed in 1969 on his third tour when Patrick was 17. "When I look at own my kids, I want them to grow up in a rush so I can be there for them," he says as he makes rubbings of his father's name for relatives back home. "The first time I came, five years ago, it was really hard. It's easier now. But I never got a chance to make peace with him."

11:04 A.M. A plane descends into National Airport, flying from the angle of the V along the horizontal line of the west side panels. Planes seem to fly in every twenty minutes, adding to the hum of tour bus engines and crickets.

11:20 A.M. A card leans against the base of the Wall. Attached to it is a photo of a young soldier in dress uniform, a service ribbon and some bits of dried palms. On the back of the card is a handwritten note: "From those of us who didn't give up their lives or limbs, but our youth—and live with the horrors and memories. We will never forget you and your families. Lance Corporal Jim McKenna, Brooklyn, NY, VAM 8/4/67 to 4/10/69." Next to the card is another snapshot, this of a soldier with a dog. On the back is handwritten: "To my dog Ralph, who never made it back."

"I left for Vietnam twenty-five years ago today," says Jim McKenna, now 45 and white haired. "That's why I'm here. Twenty-one months and six days from now, I'll be here again. That'll be twenty-five years since I came home."

It is McKenna's first trip to the Wall. "I'm here with my girlfriend, but I told her I wanted to be alone. There are many of us wondering why we're not up there and wishing we were. I came home in April of '69 and was greeted by a bunch of hippies who spat on us. And the next day in the papers they said, Crazed Marines arrive home.' They didn't say 'hippies' greet our returning veterans and spit on them.' If those people wanted somebody to take their frustration out on, they should have spat on Washington, not on me. I just went there to come back alive.

"When I came back, I withdrew, to the point that when someone I knew came up to me and said, 'Gee, I haven't seen you in years, where you been?' I told them I was away at college. I was tired of hearing, 'How does it feel to be a baby killer?' and all the other shit people said who really didn't understand. I withdrew into alcohol. I didn't use drugs, but many of the guys did, and even wound up killing themselves, one way or another, by suicide or by drugs. A good friend of mine from Chicago died last year from Agent Orange, after twenty-some years. And now he's dead. He lived through the war and came back here to die of that.

"My uncle was in World War II. He says, 'I can't relive what you lived over there, and you can't relive what I lived in World War II, but I can tell you one thing: You're going to relive it your whole life. It will never go away.' And to this day, I still have nightmares."

McKenna brought the card to the Wall, he says, "to honor these people, as tokens of my friendship and love. They are the ones who deserve the ribbons, the medals, the tribute. I just happen to be lucky enough to be able to stand here twenty-five years later and thank them for giving up something I couldn't give. It's like sending something into outer space in a capsule, so someday it will be found. I'm not looking to be remembered. These people have got to be remembered. That's why this Wall is here."

He describes the objects he left. "This is a ribbon everyone got who was lucky enough to go to Vietnam. And this is a palm from Palm Sunday. It was sent to me to protect me as a Catholic. My family thought that would help. So I carried it with me while I was in Vietnam.

"Ralph," he says, "was my dog, a mutt I found and cared for and had for maybe nine or ten months. They sent me up to Dong Ha, and the commander wouldn't let me keep her. She was pregnant, and he said she might bite somebody or might have some disease. She and I and this officer went to this village outside where we were, and I let her go, and that night we destroyed the village. I watched while we bombarded it to hell, and I think she was either eaten by the Vietnamese before the bombing, or she was killed. Then later we were going through there, and we came up to the destroyed village, and I saw all these dogs that looked like my dog, and I hated that commander. I'm still bitter about it.

"Over there, you start to imagine what it's like being here, but then you realize you're still there, and you're forgetting where you really are. Then one day you find out you're nowhere. You come back here, and people say you're not you no more, and you know it, and you can't go back there no more. So where are you? You're a nowhere man. You're left with nothing. They take a kid

out of high school, send him to boot camp, and then send him over there. I met a friend in the Marine Corps who was coming back just as I was going, and I said, 'What's it like over there?' And he said, 'You know, Jim, as kids growing up in Brooklyn, we thought of war as John Wayne running up a hill with two .45's in his hand, killing a million people and never having to reload. You're not going to really realize you're in Vietnam, and what's ahead of you, and how you're going to have to live until you're sittin' there, and talkin' to some kid from Podunk, Iowa, and telling each other your life history, and you're called out on patrol. The next thing you know, there he is laying with his face blown off in front of you. That's when you know you're in Vietnam."

11:30 A.M. At the ranger kiosk Emmelene Gura is at the computer looking up a name for Marvin McFeaters, from Falls Church, Virginia. He doesn't remember the last name of the person who died. He's looking it up for a friend. "I know he was thirty-three, and he was a Marine officer and he was killed in June. And I know his first name. Walter." McFeaters is 47, the average age of Vietnam veterans today, he says.

"I probably come to the Wall a couple times a year," says McFeaters, who also served in Vietnam. "There was a time I came a couple of times a month. I would just walk, think, meditate. One time I came down here, 8 o'clock in the morning, it was January, 1985, there was a blanket of snow over the ground. It had just snowed. And the only person out here was a fellow sweeping the walks, and me. It was a real sense of peace and quiet. It's a very safe place, a very reverential place. It's a monument for those who died, but also for those who lived. I like the fact that the living are reflected in the walls. But it is also a cemetery, in the sense that when you see somebody's name inscribed in stone, you know that he's dead. It really brings it home. There's an immediacy about it. When I saw a fellow I knew from Vietnam, it really brought it home."

"I've got two Walters," says Emmelene. She prints out the names and hands the page to McFeaters.

"The second lieutenant was born in '46," he says, "so he would only have been twenty-one at the time, so he's too young. The second one is a major, thirty-three years old, first name Walter, killed in June. Got to be him."

THE WALL

McFeaters says his friend had been engaged to this Marine named Walter. "She won't come down here," he says. "She never really got over him." He thanks Gura and walks off toward the Wall.

11:32 A.M. Lorita and Ethel Saboie, Alma Johnson and Beverly Boudoin, from Edgard, Louisiana, are in Washington for a convention of the Knights of Peter Claver and the Ladies Auxiliary. On the Wall they've found the name of Anthony Miller, a high-school classmate. "It just can't be a waste," says Lorita. "There were so many lives. It makes you think about your family, especially if you have a son."

Roger Ellis, a bearded Vietnam vet, is thinking about Ned Heath, his best friend from boot camp in Kentucky. "In 'Nam we were in different companies, but we saw each other at base camp every night. And then one night he didn't come back."

11:45 A.M. "Growing up in Brooklyn, it's so easy to say 'I'm gonna kill you,'" says Jim McKenna, unable to break away from the Wall. "You punch a kid in the nose, and he gets a bloody nose, and that's the end of it. You knock a tooth out, everybody goes home. Kids say, 'I'm gonna kill you,' but those are just words until that split second when a 13-year old girl comes runnin' out of the jungle with a machine gun and starts killin' a bunch of guys, and you're standin' there, and you have to make that decision. You're eighteen, you're brought up as a Catholic to be compassionate, 'Thou shall not kill,' and Paul says, 'Thou shall not lay hands on a woman,' and here comes a 13-year old girl with a machine gun aiming at you. All those principles, those philosophies, all that upbringing and compassion, is now out the window. Because if you think about it, you're already dead. You have these kids from the corn fields of Iowa, and now they're in Vietnam, and they're compassionate and feeling and religious, and they take a walk through a village that has just been destroyed by artillery and mortar. And there's this cradle with an infant crying in it." Long pause. "And you yell to this stupid idiot, 'Don't pick the kid up!' But he does, and it's booby trapped, and there's the end of him and the baby. These are teenagers. They forget, and they're dead, and it's too late for them. And that's the realities and horrors you live with. I saw this. They booby trapped a baby."

As he talks, Jim turns to look out over the grass in front of the Wall, his back to the monument. What is he seeing? "I'm seeing myself in a place and time where I never thought I would be twenty-five years ago. I see a man in his forties, a bitter man talking about things he hasn't told even his family or closest friends, that he hasn't told anyone in twenty-five years." He laughs. "I guess I'm a guy who came here to pay his respects, to thank them. Somebody has to.

"This wall is just a big black wall, a hole in the ground. I'm in a hole with these people on the Wall, and it seems appropriate, because I've been in a hole since I left for Vietnam twenty-five years ago today. But what I feel is unimportant. They are the ones who died."

PAUL R SETZER · FRANK R STAMPER ·
A · ARNOLD E ISON · KENNETH A ARVIDSON ·
CHESLEY · JERRY T HELLAND · JOHN E LEER ·
G TODD · WILLIAM L ARMSTRONG · SAMUEL L DELLOS ·
ROBERT L HOPKINS · PHILLIP R LOONEY ·
R Jr · JAMES W POWERS · WILLIAM J STALNECKER ·
MES B WOODS III · BRUCE G BARTH · JAMES B O'KANE ·
VILBERT R BUTLER · RALPH BYRD · GENE E CHEPELY ·
SLAND · PRINCE C CUNNINGHAM · DAVID B GARCIA ·
HERMAN L HUEY · SYLVESTER JACKSON Jr ·
ER · DERLYN R LEHMANN · KONSTANTINS A LUBAVS ·
YA · DALE R McINNIS · CLIFFORD W McROBERTS ·
SBORNE · MORRIS J POWELL · THOMAS SALAS RIVERA ·
EORGE J SHUFELT · RONALD M SNOW ·
WHITE · CLARENCE GALLOWAY · JOHN W COBB ·
IAM E HINES Jr · JOHN W OWENS · DENNIS R MARTIN ·
LL · WENDELL R WHEAT · CHARLES R WILLIAMS · ·
MSTUTZ Jr · ROBERT K LOVELACE · LESLIE H CANTRELL ·
JOHN B MECKEL · JOHN H MINCEY ·
RE · DON R SHACKELFORD · ROBERT S ANDRADE ·
ALVIN HOSKINS · RUSSELL P HUNTER Jr ·
· TEOFILO CASTILLO PIMENTEL · JOHN S VOEGTLI ·
SEBASTIAN PIADOCHE CANLAS · ROBERT O CANTRELL ·
DAVIS · SAFFORD S PYE · DANNY C SCHULTZ ·
DELANGE · RONALD W HOBBS · KENNETH R HORNE ·
ARTZ Jr · HENRY H MEASLEY Jr · THOMAS E O'NEILL Jr ·
ELER · ROGER A BISE · LEONARD D FORD ·
TER KISALA · CHARLES T PITTMAN ·
GERS · JOHN W HOUSTON · JAMES E THOMPSON ·
A C BOGGS Jr · DAVID J BOYLE · WARREN W PFEFFERLE ·
ES · LEWIS R DIETZ · CORDIE LEE DIXON ·
CAN · JOHN W O GROOVER · GEORGE E HAYES ·
PH D JARRELL · CARLOS D JELKS · DENNIS D BACKEN ·
IGAN · WILLIAM R McKIM · ELI W NICHOLS ·
DISILL · HENRY M STARKEY · ERNEST G TOMPKINS ·
LLIS · TERRY JOE REED · LADD R CONDY ·
CAR MAUTERER · ROBERT ORTOGERO NATARTE ·
ND N STEPHENSON · ANTHONY R VALENTINO ·
E · FREDDIE G LLOYD · ROSS J PATERSON ·
LEN E CARR · LUIS DE LA TORRE · GARY B GORTON ·
OBERT E LEE · JUAN A LOPEZ-COLON · HUGH A LOVE ·
ERT L SMITH · SHERDIN J WATKINS ·
ICHARD F BARNES · JOSEPH F BENTON ·
ER · GLENN V CURRY · WILLIE E DAVIS ·
AZIANO · PATRICK J HARRIS · REYNALDO R CAVAZOS ·
ES · LYELL E KING · CHRISTOPHER J LANTZ ·
DOMINIC J PREIRA Jr · WILLIAM C RIGG ·
HROEFFEL · DONALD M SHAFER II · ALBERT M SMITH ·
Jr · HURSHEL FRASURE · PAUL A GILBERT ·

KENNETH A BODELL · HAROL
DEAN A DU VALL · ALBERTO
RICHARD K JAMROS · EDWIN
MARSHALL E PAULEY · DAVID
WILEY C BIRKLAND · EARLE
ROBERT L HILTON · KARL
LIONEL RANDOLPH · DAN
STEADMON ADAMS Jr · RAY
DUANE K HEISER · ROY J
IGNACIO HUICOCHEA-R
MARTIN R SCOTT · GEOR
PEDRO VAZQUEZ-GON
MARION C BROWN · RO
CHARLES B JEFFRIES Jr ·
RONALD L REED · JERRY
CHARLIE C WALKER · JER
WILLIAM H CRAIG Jr · M
JAMES R REILLY · GORD
· THERON S DEMPSEY · JA
JOE D KELLY · RAYMON
DANIEL G STANDS Jr · R
JAMES E KEELER · ALEXA
WILLIAM E CANNON ·
MARK J GARDELLA · AR
CLIFFORD A McKENNAN
JOHN R TURNER · JOHN
DENNIS R ANDREW · T
ROBERT G BROWN · DA
· RONNIE L CONNACHER
JAMES H CAVICCHI Jr · BO
TERRY L HARPER · ROGER
NOAH M KRAFT · RAYMON
MICHAEL G MURRAY · JAM
WALTER R SHORTT · WALTE
DANIEL TIENDA · JULIUS J
PAUL R DRUMMOND · DE
EDWARD J DEVINCENT Jr ·
EDUARDO GONZALEZ ·
· JERRY M McWHORTER
RICHARD A CARUOLO ·
ISIAH FOSTER · BIENVE
EDMUND L SUDLER · JO
JAMES A DOKE · ROBERT
JOSEPH G VILLIARD · RO
JESUS A MUNOZ · CLYDE
ALLEN G LANE · ALT CHA
RICHARD A ECKVALL · HU
MICHAEL DEANE LAUX ·
SAMUEL MEDINA RAMIRE
CLARENCE A WHITEHEA

A · HOWARD W HENNINGER · JOHN H HERLIHY Jr · JAMES E HUGHES ·
GERALD E OLSON · UDON PARKER · ROBERT E PASEKOFF ·
RD D PIERCE · ROBERT A STREET · GENE L DAVIS · CYRUS S ROBERTS IV ·
ARVIN HARPER · GERALD W HEUSTON · PHIL TABB ·
MORTON · FRANK MULLEN · JAMES E PILIMAN · RICHARD F WALLACE ·
Y RAY SLADE · RANDALL S HICKMAN · ROBERT L TAYLOR ·
LUCCI · DON W CHABOT · THOMAS J CHANDLER Jr · ROBERT L DIAL ·
LIAM R HOLBROOK · DAVID H HOLMES · RAYMOND HOOD ·
ASH · HERMAN PENN · GARY E BARTZ · CARMELO SANCHEZ-BERRIOS ·
· ALLAN STEGALL Jr · PETER F STEWART · DORSEY L TATUM ·
VILLIAMS · GEORGE W ABEY · WILLIAM H HUBBARD · CHARLES A BELL ·
VILLIAM O GOSSETT · JOHN H BEAUCHAMP Jr · JAMES K HUGHES ·
NETH M KNUDSON · JERRY D LEWIS · CURTIS C NICKERSON ·
ICHARD F SMITH · WILLIAM N THOMPSON · PAUL G UNDERWOOD ·
HARLES A ZIONTS · JACK L NEIDRICK · ALBERT K CHRISTY ·
F · BENJAMIN LEE IV · VIRGIL A MURRAY · GARLAND C BOBBITT ·
NNIE M TENON · FRANCIS W CLARK · BRENT E DAVIS ·
GASTON D GODFREY · DALLAS E HICKMAN · THOMAS F HORNBY ·
TT A McPHERSON · ENRICO H PAGNANO Jr · JIMMIE TAVY SMILEY ·
· JAMES S WILLIAMS · ROBERT H CORLEY · MARK FERRELL Jr ·
JIMMIE L WALLACE Jr · JAMES P WILLIAMS · MARVIN F GOODMAN Jr ·
DENNIS D FERGUSON · THEODORE L FISCHER · DAVID FLORES ·
HARD A GROOVER · GEORGE HITZELBERGER · TOMMIE L McFARLAND ·
ER · JOHN H SAVAGEAU · GERALD B SCHMIDT · HUBERT R SMITH ·
SSY RAY WANGLER · ROY R ALLEN · LOUIS A AMBROSE ·
USSELL E BISHOP · WILLIAM C BLANCHARD · JOHN M BOWERS ·
ARD J FRIESE · CALVIN K CHOW · FRANK R COMPTON ·
· JOSEPH B ELARNO · THOMAS B FLOOD · JOHN H FRANKLIN ·
E · MARTIN L GILLESPIE Jr · MARVIN E GLASSBURN · GAROLD A HANN ·
ANUEL HERRERA · JOHN L HUNTER · BENITO IGARTA Jr ·
STEPHAN J MARTIN · LESTER G MICHELS · JOHN A MITCHELL ·
Y LEE QUINN · STANLEY RIFFLE · JOHN F SCULL Jr · WILLIAM K SHOUP ·
LLIAM A STACY Jr · RICHARD D SWAYZE · JOHN M TIDERMAN ·
M G WADE · BRUCE L WATKINS · HAROLD W WILSON ·
WILLIAM E BURKE III · JOHNNIE M CURLEE · MICHAEL I DELGADO Jr ·
LE · JESSE G EASTMAN · FRANK R ESCH · ARNOLD J FAULKNER ·
ARD · BRUCE R LANDIS Jr · JERRY D LEE · MARION L LEE Jr ·
O · JOHN C ROBERTSON · RAYMOND W WILSON · FRED Y WRIGHT Jr ·
J · DONALD E CLARK Jr · CLYDE D DAWSON · SAMUEL E HEWITT ·
A · GEORGE P KING · JEROME NIXON · RONALD A SAPP ·
TE BUSH · GENERAL WHITE · JAMES M CORNETT · CHARLES E DANIELS ·
AEL M JACKSON · CARL H JOYNER · ALBERT M KEEN Jr ·
AAS VASQUEZ MARTINEZ · JOSEPH A MASON Jr · LEONARD D MAY ·
LD SCHATZLEY · CARL R SMEAD · ROBERT E URBANOVSKY ·
OPELAND II · CHARLES HARMON · ANTONIO QUICHOCHO SABLAN ·
RICHARD M EPPS · JAMES V DONNELLY · THOMAS K KING ·
CLYDE D McDONALD II · RONALD M NEUMAN · SHIRLEY W O'BOYLE ·
NSON · CHARLES N RUDD · PATRICK M DOYLE · JOHN B SHERMAN ·
NDRE · CHARLES T COURSON · RICHARD K HILL · JAMES L HUDSPETH ·

EDWARD D
SAMUEL H
RAMON A P
ANDRA CUN
JERRY W R SA
TOMMY LEE
JOSEPH AGU
DAVID G U
JAMES A LEV
WILLIAM M
JOSE F RIVER
JULIAN B W
EDWARD R L
GEORGE T S
JOHN J CARV
ALBERT M SI
KENNETH E L
RONNIE E M
ANTONINE
FRED L RICH
JOSEPH A SC
JOHN A BRO
CARY CRAD
RUSSELL H A
MALAKIA JA
JERRY RAY M
EARNEST A T
WILBERT I AN
THOMAS D
GEORGE L SI
ROBERT L BO
JOAQUIN D
LEONARD F
JOSEPH C M
JOSEPH H R
WILLIAM S
OWEN W W
HERMANDO
MICHAEL LI
EDWARD R L
JOHN E CAIL
KEITH R KNO
JOHN E BAIL
TEE W DECK
WILLIE J PEI
TOM L AUS
ANDREW W
HAROLD L D
MARK L WI

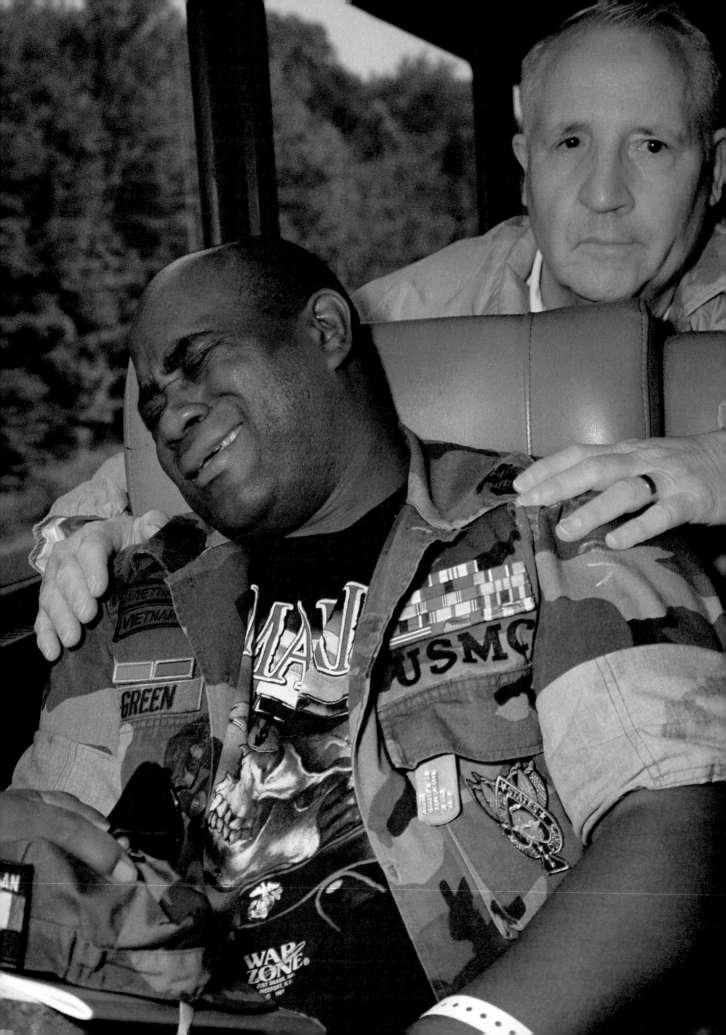

4. A LONG AND LONESOME HIGHWAY

12:00 Noon John Obenchain, a yellow cap Episcopal priest, is fingering his soldiers' directory with one hand, his walkie-talkie with the other. "A group of vets is coming from Pennsylvania," he says. Everyone official on site knows about the arrival. At the Wall veterans are special. Obenchain was in seminary "when Vietnam was cooking," but comes to the Wall twice a month, from his home in Oxford, Pennsylvania. He does a lot of listening, he says, hears a lot of sad stories. He stays at the Wall round the clock on the heavy days such as Memorial Day and Veterans Day. "I had a buddy who was in the Marines and it was part of his therapy to come down to the Wall," he says. "So I got interested, too." His wife, a nurse who works with PTSD veterans, will be on the Pennsylvania bus. The walkie-talkie squawks. "They're on their way," says Obenchain. "The bus just pulled in."

12:05 P.M. It's dead quiet on board the big red, white and blue bus. For the 30 nervous Vietnam War veterans staring out the window, this is it. The Wall—the gash of memory that has tortured them for over two decades.

On the trip down Bob Green woke from a nap screaming. It was a primal sound, like a child's wordless cry for help. "I was remembering," said Green. "Back then, things were kind of rough, especially when your own people were shooting at you. One morning, just after I got up, a piece of shrapnel landed right on my pillow. I would have been dead. You never knew if you were going to make it back or not." Tears ran down his dark face. "We lost two guys in my platoon. To me it's like yesterday."

As the bus rolled into Washington—an American flag pasted to a window in the rear and "VA Medical Center, Coatesville, PA," prominently painted on the side—passersby stopped to look. Many waved. The men's spirits were buoyed. Was this the welcome home they never received?

Bob Green and the other men on the bus are among the thousands of walking wounded from the war. They have PTSD. Twenty-five years after their war and they still can't nap without nightmares.

"There are certain set patterns for PTSD," says Dr. Steven M. Silver, a Vietnam vet and director of the Coatesville program. "They include nightmares, obtrusive memories and flashbacks. Smashed up relationships, a long history of jobs—twenty, thirty, forty, fifty jobs since they got out of the service, isolation, withdrawal from people, and the inability to maintain any kind of relationship, are common."

The Coatesville hospital has one of the oldest PTSD inpatient units in the country, started in 1982, two years after the American Psychiatric Association designated PTSD as a clinical disorder. There are now 20 similar programs which have treated tens of thousands of veterans with severe emotional reactions to combat. According to the VA, as many as 15 percent of the three million U.S. men and women who served in the Southeast Asian war zone have had PTSD.

"I was around too many explosions," says Bob Green. "I'm always going to sleep with one eye open, one eye closed. You got to know the difference between the sound of a round coming in and a round going out. Last night I stood straight up in my bed like I was there."

Silently, the men from Coatesville file out into the dazzling Washington sun, fazed momentarily by the heat and humidity and then by the crowds. The drive in front of the ranger kiosk is teeming with tourists, vendors, other vets. And almost as quickly as they are off the bus, the men try to disappear into the crowds. They do not want to be associated with "the mental hospital." They do not want to be seen as crazies.

George Dye and Rick Pierce unload a pine-bough wreath from the belly of the bus. With Willie Jordan and Bob Christina, in his wheelchair, they begin the slow trek to the vertex of the Wall.

Dye, 42, who is married and has four children, has been in several VA programs for PTSD. "I wasn't aware what was going on in me for the longest time. Then one night I woke up, I was on the floor—like shooting Charlie [North Vietnamese soldiers]. I had employment problems. I was belligerent at work. I had drinking problems. I thought it was normal. How would I know it wasn't?"

Jordan, 45, who served in the Army's 4th Infantry, says,

"Everything was going backwards in my life after the war. Then the bottom just falls out. And you can't figure out why."

"These are not crazy people," says Silver, who has come with his men to the Wall. "They are not dysfunctional psychotics. These are normal people. They've just been through things that normal people shouldn't have to go through."

Passing the statue of the three soldiers, the Wall comes into view. Dye's eyes catch it and for what seems like several missteps he can't stop looking. Jordan sees it a moment later and he, too, is transfixed. A park ranger approaches the foursome, three of whom are smoking, and announces, "No smoking down at the Wall." They are back on track.

They move cautiously but single-mindedly down the path. Amidst the clutter of tourists, they reach the vertex, placing the wreath gently in front of the panel dated 1959. In a matter of moments the wreath is just another testimonial left at the Wall. Its centerpiece consists of two flags, one of the U.S. and one in remembrance of POW-MIAs (You Are Not Forgotten). A plaque has been signed by every man on the PTSD unit:

"In Honor and Memory With Gratitude
PTSD Unit 59B
Coatesville, Pa.
Veterans Hospital
August 4, 1992"

Dye stands back and stares down at the wreath, giving it a silent salute. Then he slowly melts into the crowd.

12:29 P.M. Psychologist Bob Whitney's group of nine has made little progress in approaching the Wall. Whitney, one of five therapists on the bus, has been coaxing his men forward, but after nearly half an hour they remain stuck near the circle at the soldiers statue.

At 12:31, Rick Cullinan, a 40-year-old bearded ex-Marine "grunt," puts on his fatigue coat. Despite the heat, he wants to be respectfully dressed. Every man is carrying an American flag. Slowly and together, Cullinan, Frank Ham, Bob Stouch, Lester Kearney, Dave Young, Harry Bonella, Charlie Williams, Bob Stouch, Nyoke Snowden and Bob Whitney start off. The war still lives in them. It's in their eyes, rubbed ragged from crying, unfocused from years, even decades, of pain. Mostly, you can see it in the way they walk: their bodies hung over from two decades of shame and death.

Lester Kearney, married five times since his one-year

tour of duty, remains plagued—no, consumed—by an act of kindness that for reasons entirely out of his control resulted in a death sentence. Kearney, then a sergeant in the 25th Infantry Division, ordered a soldier in his command to go take a rest before his next maneuvers. "I told him to go down there," Kearney explained. "And then he was ambushed. He died. I killed him. He was my friend and I loved him, and I dream about him all the time." After the war Kearney became an alcohol and drug abuser. "I don't understand why him and not me. It keeps hurting," he said. "As a commanding officer, I couldn't show forty other people too much weakness. I didn't get a chance to say goodbye or to pay my respects. I couldn't say, 'I love you.'" Kearney begins to lose his words and choke on his tears. "I feel like I betrayed his friendship. I feel like I owe him my life. I wish I could just pay the price—my heart or my soul—so I wouldn't have to keep feeling this."

After a long pause, Kearney said quietly, "I lost a lot of buddies." And he began a roll call of the dead: "Johnson, Snyder, Starns, Olds.... They all got killed."

Says Rick Cullinan, another veteran who can't sleep at night, "I would use speed to stay awake because I was afraid to go to sleep. Then I'd use alcohol to go to sleep." Cullinan still smokes four packs of cigarettes a day. "I don't like to be that way. I want that confidence back we had when were in Vietnam."

But for the Philadelphia native and father of one who hasn't worked in ten years, there's a lot more to his Vietnam experience than confidence, and it's only since the Coatesville program that he is beginning to remember some of what he was trying so hard to forget. "We had hired this boy to show us where booby traps were. And I remember seeing him blown up by accident one day. His hair was all gone and his skin was ripped off. But most of all I can't forget the scream when the mine went off." Catching his breath, he continues slowly and ends shaking his head, mouthing, "the screaming, the screaming. They put him on a chopper and that's the last I heard. The screaming."

"These guys have been running like outlaws since the war, pretty much alone and feeling like no one understands them," says psychologist Silver. Some 90 percent of the vets in the program have been substance abusers, he explains. Only one-quarter are still married, half of them have children. Most have been married more than once and for many, he says, "This is their last best chance to save their marriages before they lose their wives and kids.... They need a place like this, where guys have had similar experiences and are working on the same kinds of issues. There's instant identification."

And going to the Wall is a regular part of the treatment program, says Silver. In fact, many VA hospitals, American Legion groups and store-front vet centers regularly schedule therapeutic trips to the Wall. Dr. Arthur Blank, Director of the Veterans Readjustment Counseling Centers in Washington and a Vietnam veteran himself, says, "The ritual of going to the memorial is very healing for vets with PTSD or just with unfinished emotional business." Silver, who has been to the Wall more than 60 times, says, "The Wall is like a Rorschach test. It allows people to project onto it whatever it is they're carrying around."

"It don't get any easier no matter how many times you go," says Rick Cullinan, who had been to the Wall before and hoped to be a shoulder for the men who were visiting for the first time.

But the day before the trip, as apprehension increased, none of the veterans was feeling confident. "I'm really scared and nervous," said Bob Stouch, a father of three who had once been an Army Airborne Ranger, one of the toughest assignments in the business.

"You run so long," said Frank Ham, a big man wearing a *Vietnam Veteran and Proud of It* cap. "You hide so long that you don't know what you're hiding from. Once you face the Wall, you've got to deal with it." There was a gentle nodding of heads to show Ham had spoken a truth. "Without this program, we wouldn't have a chance," he continued. "I've never been to the Wall before, and I'm scared of going. If I wasn't in this program, I wouldn't go."

Charles Williams, a veteran of three tours of duty, caught Stouch's eye: "Coming from a mental hospital, I don't want to be perceived as crazy." He stopped for a breath, and then added, "But I guess we are in some way."

For days before the trip they tried to buck each other up.

Says Cullinan: "I just want to go down and sit and talk to my friends. I believe they are there. They gave up the ultimate sacrifice. I just want to thank them." And then: "I also want to heal some of the pain in my life."

After only ten yards, Frank Ham begins to cry, softly at first, but within moments the 6' 2" one-time machine gunner who did two tours of duty and earned three Purple Hearts, has broken down, and begins sobbing and then weeping as he puts his arms around an oak tree and tries to pull himself into it.

Before coming to this program Ham had cried only once in his adult life, and that was his first night in Vietnam when he was sent out into the jungle and got hit. Of his two years in Vietnam, Ham says, "I got older, but I didn't grow up. Like the others, I came back a shell. I got drunk to have no memory or feelings. I'm afraid I'm gonna remember things. I'm afraid that I'm going to remember the names of people who were killed." He is trembling. The years since the war have not been good to Ham. He has no home, no family, no job. "I was trying not to be the guy from Vietnam. I tried to hide my identity. I even hid my uniform. I didn't fit in anywhere." And then one night, Ham's rage boiled over. He got in a fight and sent a man to the hospital, where he developed pneumonia and died.

"Please forgive me, please forgive me," he now sobs over and over as Bob Whitney gives him a long hug. In a matter of moments the other men are hugging Ham as well. Everyone is crying, and confusion seems to reign until a band of tourists—with cameras and camcorders —approaches. The men quickly retreat into themselves.

"We're going down," Dave Young says to the others. They start again. This time they make it. Even Frank Ham, who gets past 24,000 dead before he has to turn back.

Lester Kearney has broken away from the group to look for his cousin's name on panel E7 and to read him the two-paragraph letter that took him over four hours to write. With his own reflection staring back at him from the black wall, Kearney methodically counts the lines down until, to his surprise, the name of Preston John Snyder actually appears in the stone. As he unfolds the letter, he sweats profusely in the midday sun; then he starts to tear up. He is holding an American flag in one hand, the letter in the other. "Dear John," he begins quietly. "Forgive me for not saying goodbye, forgive me for not being brave enough to ask you for your forgiveness!" He is stumbling, his eyes blurred by the waterfall

of tears. "I know I could never live up to your bravery but there is only one thing you must know! I LOVE you and I am sorry for the deed I couldn't undo. Brother, forgive me please. Your friend forever, Lester Kearney."

Then Kearney takes his thumb and slowly rubs it back and forth over Snyder's name, trying somehow to slip his finger into the Wall and be one again. Kearney places the letter and the flag down, unfurls the flag, kneels down and asks for forgiveness. From a short distance, all you can see is the back of this warrior stooped and sobbing, desperately trying to find his own peace.

Steve Silver is there with a warm embrace as Kearney gets up. "Thank you," Lester says to him as they hold each other. A baby cries out nearby. Lester walks the rest of the way past the other dead by himself. He stops one more time, to say goodbye to his friend Myron S. Beech, Jr., and then moves on, finally victorious.

12:40 P.M. "It gives them something to remember that they've been here," says Chris Sprock, a tourist from Michigan watching one of the veterans execute a name rubbing. "Such strong memories, so many years after." This is Sprock's first visit to the Wall. She wasn't prepared for the strong emotions. "I thought you just kind of walked by," she says solemnly. "I didn't expect to see all these people stopping and tracing names. And the number of names, it's just really sad."

12:45 P.M. The flow of visitors is constant. The yellow caps are spread out among the crowd, looking up names, handing out paper and pencil, answering questions. They go up ladders to do rubbings.

One of the Coatesville men, Ray Stanfield, in an army jacket covered with pins and patches, stands silently in front of a name on the Wall. With his watery blue eyes and pale skin shaded by a camouflage hat, he has the look of someone who has been permanently saddened. He had three tours of duty between 1965 and 1971, three years and three months in all. Many of his friends were killed. This is his third visit to the Wall. "It gives me peace to visit my comrades, my brothers and sisters," he says. "It's a way to say hello. I love it, and I hate it, too. More than fifty-eight thousand died for no just reason. We were doing a heck of a job, and we weren't allowed to finish it. As it was, we caught hell for it."

Stanfield ponders his friend's name. "I see him looking out at me, just there, telling me it's all right." He pauses, then says, "It's very hard to adjust."

12:54 P.M. A group of young kids from a local day camp are taking rubbings. "Ralph Blackenbury...You know what I'm gonna do? I'm gonna just...Ralph Blackenbury...I need another piece of paper... Oh, watch out!... I can't get this one... I got mine... I got one... Where'd I see that name at?...I'm keepin' this..."

Says one young boy: "I took a big name. Ralph Blackenbury. This is the first time I came. It's big!"

1:00 P.M. Bob Stouch stands in front of the name of his cousin, Harry J. Moser. It is Stouch's first visit to the memorial. "I was overwhelmed at first," he says, "but it feels good to see all the names. It makes me feel proud to be a vet for the first time in twenty years."

Stouch has been at the Coatesville hospital since May. "I always saw pictures in my head of people dying," he says. "One day last spring I found myself out in the backyard chasing Vietnamese devils with a hatchet. I thought they were after my kids [he has three]. But I couldn't catch them, they kept eluding me, they'd be in one tree and then another. My wife found me and she started crying and saying 'You need help, you've got to get help.' So that's when I knew I had to do something. I hadn't been able to get close to my family, I couldn't let them love me because I thought I wasn't worthy. You see, there was this baby—"

These are real demons. "We were out on one of these search-and-destroy missions," he says. "We came across a VC village, and they all took off, but they left a baby there. It had sores all over it, and it had a big belly. It was sick and it was dying. I wanted to take it home. I wanted to hug it. I love kids. I would never hurt a kid. Even if I saw a kid with a hand grenade coming at me, I think I'd run if I could. I just couldn't kill a kid. . ." Stouch has only recently been able to tell this story. "But I knew I had to kill it," he says flatly. "There was just nothing else we could do. I didn't want to leave it there to starve to death. And I couldn't take it. So I took my 45 out and put it at the baby's head—I couldn't do it. And neither could anybody else." But they did call in the artillery. "They blew the hut up." For several moments Stouch says nothing. Then: "That was the turning point."

1:10 P.M. A Japanese tour group of kids barrels through at a strong clip. They don't stop.

A mustachioed, middle-aged man in stylish blue shorts and a blue shirt is crying, trying to focus his camera on a name on panel 4W. After a friend comforts him, Dennis Purgatori finally takes a picture, then does a rubbing of the name: Danny G. Drinkard. "He was my best friend in the whole world," Dennis says. "We were buddies from little boys through high school. I went to college

and he went to the war." Dennis sniffs, and wipes his face again. "He was killed in April, 1971. He was Nineteen. Just got married, before he went over. He had two kids." Dennis lives in Sterling Heights, just outside of Detroit. This is his first visit, something he's been meaning to do for a long time. "It takes a lot to come here," he says, "but it was worth it. Brings back a lot of good memories, you know? Kids growing up, high school, played ball together. Lived near each other. I just had to come see him. Make sure he knows that I was here."

1:40 P.M. Everyone from the Coatesville bus is spent. Spent from the heat. Spent from the crowds. Spent from their grief. Lunch is served VA-style, which is to say it's a brown bagger: corned beef on white bread, two small cartons of orange juice, an orange and two cookies.

Rick Cullinan speaks up. "I finally made it to the far end of the Wall. It was one more step to getting me back in society."

Harry Bonella: "Today was quite a strain, I couldn't find the names of the people I was looking for.... The hurt's still there. Maybe with time it won't hurt as bad?" he asks, and with that begins to cry.

Frank Ham has barely recovered. "I feel I was unworthy. These guys gave their lives, and I'm still walking around." He pauses for several moments, trying to collect his thoughts. And then his face brightens: "But I was alive again. *I felt again.* I'm glad you guys were there. Thank you, everybody."

LaRue Smith, awakened by another nightmare, says his dream has set him to remembering again. He has a notebook that he has titled in precise letters: "Things I'd Rather Not Remember." He starts to read from his list:

> Killing two children in a ditch with a white phosphorous grenade after receiving sniper fire.

> Wounded 26 or 28th of July 1968 by incoming 82 mm mortar round shrapnel at Duc Hoa.

> Three times nearly overrun at Boa Tri near the Cambodian border, can remember just shooting and shooting and in each case after dawn all the bodies, the blood, the Vietnamese ARVN soldiers, and U.S. soldiers cutting off ears collecting souvenirs. It was Enough! Enough! *ENOUGH!*

1:50 P.M. The weather is turning weird, appropriate to the stories being told at the Wall. A thunderstorm is about to break out of the dark sky. The Coatesville veterans take time for a last smoke before boarding their bus. When everyone is on, the doors close, the air conditioning roars, and the bus lurches forward, into the storm. Dr. Silver says to the group, "I think we made some progress today."

But there is little talk in the bus. Walkmen go on. Caps are pulled down. Hands rest loose on laps. For the time being, peace, or what must pass for peace, has settled in.

"At first I felt sorrow and then as I looked at all the names, I felt deep loss," says Dave Young. "This time I finally got to say goodbye to a friend. I'm a little more at peace now."

5. THE STORM BREAKS

2:00 P.M. Rangers Lucas and Smith pick up mementos left along the Wall. They normally collect them twice a day, in the morning and at midnight, but because of the film crew, they missed the morning sweep. They leave the flowers and flags. Most items deposited at the Wall are flowers—roses, carnations, lilies, wreaths—and are thrown away after they wilt. Flags are donated to various civic organizations, unless a note or something personalized is attached.

Lucas and Smith leave the Coatesville wreath, but pick up five items, including Jim McKenna's card and picture. Each one is entered onto a list with a description and a panel number, assigned a number and dropped into a Ziploc bag. Artifact numbers are assigned according to the month and the order they are picked up. McKenna's card and picture become artifact 8/67, standing for the 67th object picked up in August. The other four objects picked up are sealed letters, which are collected but not opened.

Eventually, the collected items are transferred to the Museum And Archaeological Regional Storage facility (MARS), a sprawling Park Service warehouse outside of Washington that houses collections from 40 different national historic sites. MARS has 25,000 items from the Vietnam Veterans Memorial alone, making for one of the most unusual collections of them all. "Normally history is written from the top down rather than from the bottom up," says Duery Felton, the curator of the Vietnam Veterans Memorial Collection at MARS. "This is a social history of the common man." Diaries, photo albums, comments about individuals who are on the Wall. This collection consists of 360 degrees of uncensored commentary.

Most of the contributions are anonymous: Notes saying, "Thanks, Bobby," signed "Sarge." Felton periodically puts out calls for anonymous donors to call the collection and divulge who they are (names are kept confidential by the NPS whether a donor requests it or not) and why they left what they did. (Donors may write to MARS, P.O. Box 434, Glendale, MD, 20769, attn: Duery Felton.) This is so the curators can solve some of the mysteries of the Wall. Who left two walnuts in their shells and why? Or this: an elaborately built shadow box with a combat infantryman's badge, parachuter's wings, a package of Beech Nut peppermint gum, a government issue P 38 can opener, a toothbrush, a flag, the insignia of the 73rd Airborne Brigade and the identity of the casualty: Jimmy Dolan, Scituate, Mass., age 23. It was a donor who explained why a Cleveland *Plain Dealer* newspaper bag was left with a note written on it in an indelible marking pen: "To Pat Mooney. Remembering a sweeter gentler time period. We never dreamed serving the people would end this way. God bless you. Rest in peace. C.A.F." The community, the donor explained, had a tradition of passing along a newspaper route. One of the boys in line got sent to Vietnam and was killed before he got the route—and the bag was passed to him.

Mike Lucas has seen a Medal of Honor and thousands of other medals left at the Wall; lots of combat boots; lipstick kisses pressed on paper; kids' drawings. The most moving objects for Lucas are the model cars, boats and houses. "What gets me is when a guy is in a foxhole and dreams about things, like getting a new car—a blue Corvette, say—and he tells his buddy, `I'm gonna get me a blue Corvette when I get home.' Then he gets killed. Later, his buddy brings a toy car to the Wall, a little blue Corvette, the car his friend never got to have."

2:05 P.M. The heat has thinned out the crowd. But dozens of visitors still move slowly along the Wall, running their hands over the etched names; some just feeling the stone, others searching for people they knew, people they loved. They pass by a gray-haired man wearing slacks, short-sleeved shirt and tie, who stands alone, staring for long minutes at the Wall, cradling his face in his hand. Occasionally an excited voice is heard, "There he is," as though the person, and not just a name, is present. Cold in appearance, the Wall is warm to the touch. There seems to be a yearning to feel the one who's gone, and, once touched, his or her survivors move.

2:15 P.M. Finally, the dark skies open. When it hits, the downpour quickly scatters the crowd. People run toward trees, the ranger kiosk, the Lincoln Memorial. They line the veterans' t-shirt booths and stand under the ranger kiosk overhang. Ranger Donnie Smith shouts after them, "It's a big thunderstorm, folks. I suggest you go for cover—but NOT by standing under the trees." A few people stay at the Wall—without rain gear—getting wet.

2:35 P.M. Two figures crouch by the far east end of the memorial, drenched by the downpour but determined to find a name on the Wall. Evelyn Lahman, 52, is with her 17-year-old son, John Russell. They are the only people at the Wall in the desolate storm. Evelyn is so wet her spine is visible through the shirt that seems glued to her back.

"This was our destination," she says, "rain or no rain."

After finding her cousin's name on the Wall, she leaves—only to come back a few minutes later and lean, in tears, against the wet granite.

3:00 P.M. Steam rises from the pathway stone and rivulets of water spill off the top of the Wall onto the panels, running over the names, darkening the letters. "It looks like it's crying," says Thomas Bowman, 21, a student from the University of Michigan. The rain pours down his face, matting his blond hair, soaking his gray t-shirt, mixing with his own tears.

The Wall also looks naked. Exposed, as men in combat are exposed.

3:10 P.M. Henry and Rose Sugai are wearing plastic grocery bags over their heads. Japanese-Americans from Los Angeles, they are looking for the son of a friend of theirs—the first third-generation Japanese-American killed in Vietnam: Skyler Lance Hasuike. "His father and I went to internment camp together," says Henry. "We also fought in World War II together."

Thunder crashes as they speak, and the rain continues.

3:15 P.M. A half-dozen soaking-wet people stay at the Wall. One man is counting up from the bottom of a panel. He wears a Desert Storm t-shirt. A woman, Nancy Mahler, leads her children along the wet side-walk. She didn't know anybody on the Wall, she says, "But it is very moving, very beautiful. Living in Hawaii, our kids are not exposed much to United States history. We're so far removed from this part of the world.

"I still have mixed emotions about the war. But I think kids need to know the cost that we have paid for the freedoms that we have. We visited Gettysburg and it was moving. Just to see what it means to live in a free country. Even though I still have mixed feelings, this"—she nods toward the Wall—"this was also part of the price for living in this country and being American. It was an expensive war, and wrong not to have come out

victorious, not to have called these guys heroes or to have paid them their due."

3:30 P.M. Sharon Evoy, from La Grande, Oregon, crouches by the Wall, writing a note to Ed O'Donovan, a childhood friend from Chicago whose name is etched in granite. She was here a year ago, but didn't have time to find his name—it bothered her for the whole year. "We were just friends, not boyfriend and girlfriend. He died in 1969, when he was nineteen. I left Chicago in 1975, but I go back to some places Ed and I used to go to, like the park where we carved our names on a bridge. I just wrote him a letter and told him about the neighborhood and the park.... He was just a really nice guy. He never got to grow up. You know how men don't look like adults until they're twenty-five or so? Well, he never even got to look like an adult."

3:33 P.M. Vietnam veteran Chuck Hayden is on his knees before a low panel on the east wing, weeping. His young son Joey stands beside him, with his hand on his father's shoulder. Hayden has a gray beard and short ponytail, a much different man from the kid who went off to war a couple decades ago. "I was looking at Patrick Alfonzo Lucero," he says. "The night before he went in the Army, he and I went out and got drunk, drank a gallon of cheap red wine and partied. We partied all through high school. And he was the first one in my school to get killed." Hayden is crying. "It's like I put it off for ten years to come here. It's hard. People with PTSD don't have emotions like normal people have emotions. We learned in 'Nam twenty-three years ago to bury them. Not to have emotions when you see people die. I'm coming here and seeing people that died right with me. Right beside me."

When the Wall was first going up, Hayden didn't pay much attention. "Now I feel numb. These were just kids. We were eighteen and nineteen years old and didn't know shit from Shinola.... Fifty-eight thousand people gave their lives. It's astronomical, it's unbelievable. I graduated from high school in Annandale, Virginia, and used to come over here when this was all level. They called the reflecting ponds urinal pools cause that's where everybody'd take a leak. They had a shantytown built right here when Martin Luther King was around. I don't know if I'd rather see the shanties or see this. It's a helluva tradeoff. I mean, what do you do? I mean, you know, God knew I was coming here today because the minute I pulled up here it started raining like hell. And ninety percent of these guys here died in the rain and the mud. So this is just a shadow, a small fragment of the terror and the anguish and the hurt that people had."

Hayden decides to take a rubbing, and finds volunteer

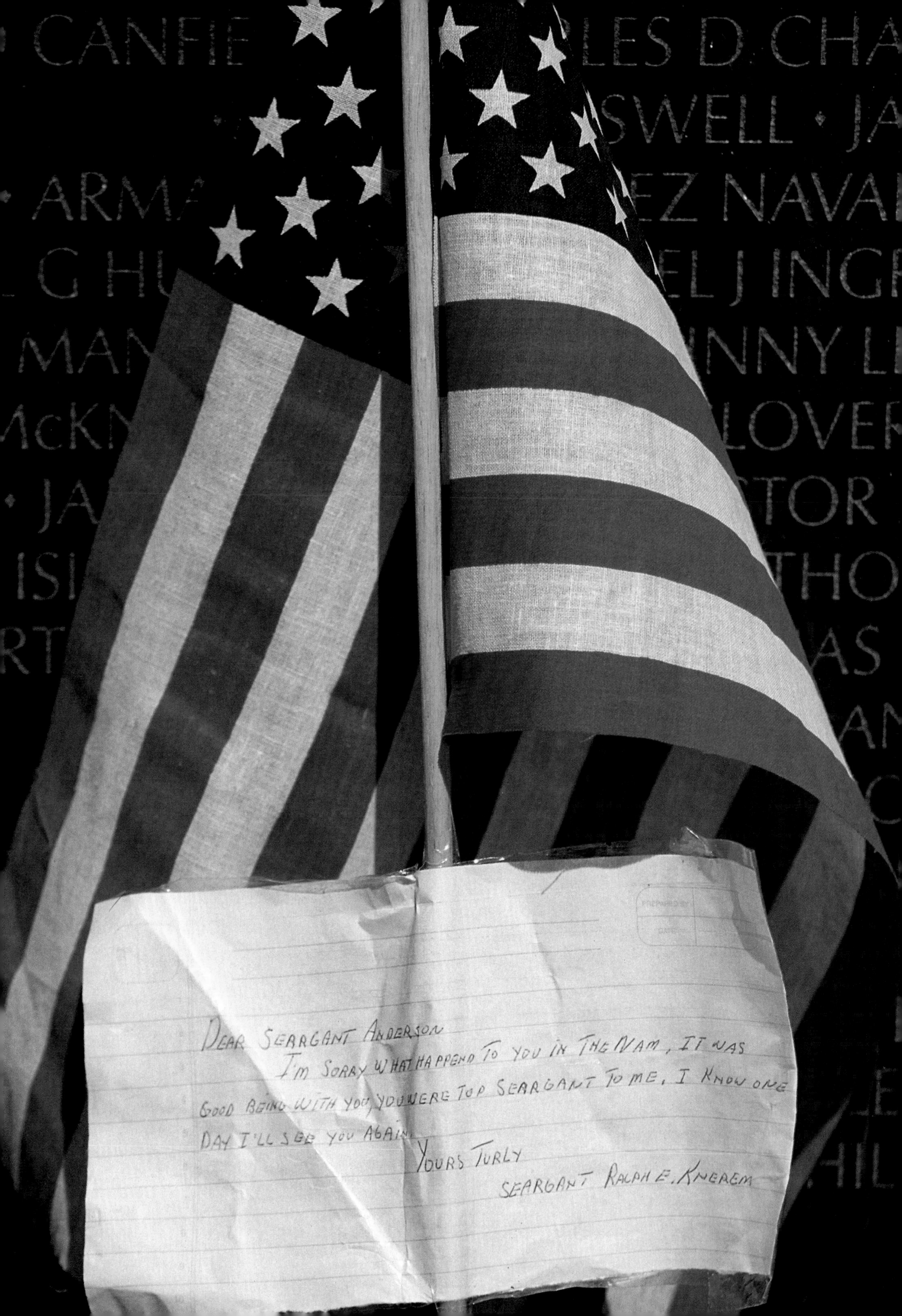
DEAR SEARGANT ANDERSON
I'M SORRY WHAT HAPPEND TO YOU IN THE NAM, IT WAS
GOOD BEING WITH YOU, YOU WERE TOP SEARGANT TO ME, I KNOW ONE
DAY I'LL SEE YOU AGAIN.
YOURS TURLY
SEARGANT RALPH E. KNEREM

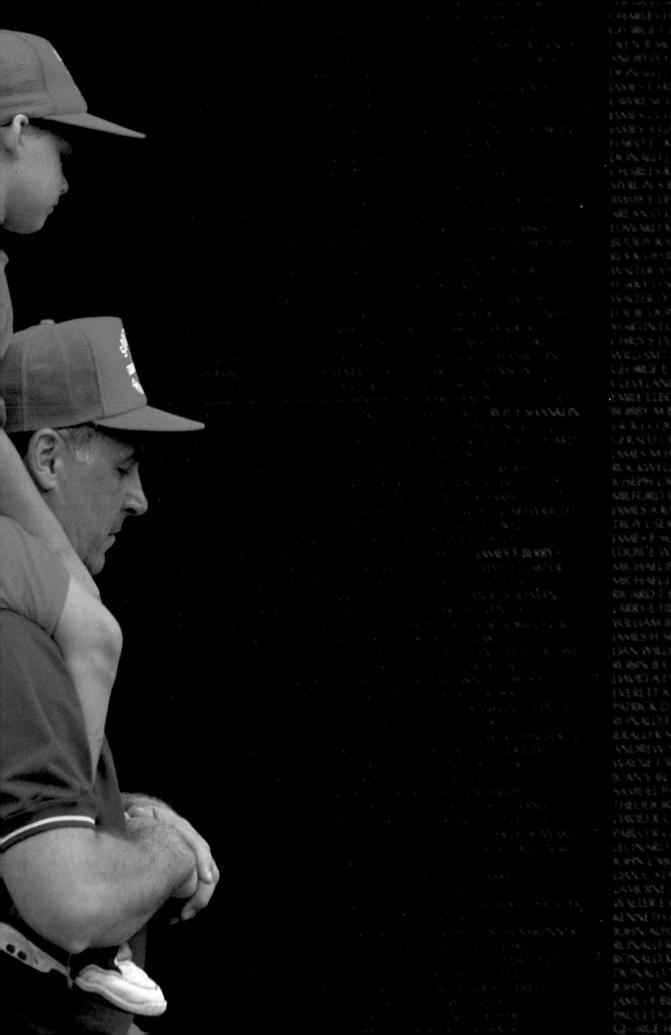

Emmelene Gura, who has paper and pencil. "How much does it cost?" he asks, pulling out a wad of bills.

"You don't pay for anything down here, sir," she tells him.

"I don't mind paying," Hayden whispers.

"Well, you don't, though," Gura says, almost roughly. "Where's your name?"

"Charles Hayden."

"No, where's the name that you want rubbed off?" she asks, gently.

"I want, ah, Pat, ah, Lucero," he says and starts to weep.

After Emmelene gives him the paper, she says, "You owe me something."

Hayden looks at her, confused.

"You owe me a hug," Gura says. The volunteer and the veteran hug.

3:40 P.M. A young woman says, "He was my cousin. It was a long time ago. I was just a teenager.... Yes, he was important to me—he taught me how to dance."

A couple in their fifties stands restlessly opposite a panel, seemingly unsure about what to do in front of the name they came to honor. The man daubs his eyes with a handkerchief, takes a picture of the name, walks back to his wife, daubs his eyes again.

Finally, he rubs the name on panel 19E, line 48, Curtis E. Chase. He lays a light blue envelope containing a large greeting card and note at the base of the Wall. The note was carefully addressed to Curtis Chase, Hingham, Massachusetts. It reads: "The skating on the pond in winter, the hunting for frogs in summer, the bike rides up and down Garrison Road, the visits to Mr. MacGoldrick's garage, the romps through the cornfield and the games played in the apple orchard—these memories will not ever be forgotten. I am sad that you are gone, but you will always be in my heart for your ultimate sacrifice. I hope that you are at peace and that God will always be at your side. Love and peace, Steve."

4:00 P.M. The sun has roared back out. It's hot again. The Wall is already dry. Matt Mays, 16, from Atlanta, touches it, leans against it with his fingers. "It's great," he says. "This is our first time in Washington. This is the only thing I really wanted to see. In sixth grade we had to do a research project on it. I never knew it was this

big. I thought it was twenty feet. I didn't know it was this many people."

4:02 P.M. The monument is still crowded. There are tourists from everywhere: Texas, California, Europe, Asia, even Harvard, Illinois.

Mike Addirusio, 42, from Killingworth, Connecticut, says he went through the draft lottery in 1968. "My number was 245. I was relieved, though I had friends who came up with higher numbers who wanted to go. One friend came up with number three, and he was ecstatic. They all came back so different. I sometimes think about how different my life would have been. It all came down to a number being drawn. This decided whose lives got ruined, and whose didn't."

4:05 P.M. Virgie Hurst, 76, from Aurora, Nebraska, was a draft board clerk from 1956 to 1973, almost the entire length of the war. "Five or ten boys a month turned eighteen, and I was in charge of notifying them, sending their orders. Not all were drafted," she said. But incredibly, "None of the youngsters I helped process are on the Wall."

4:20 P.M. Another lull in the passing parade. An older volunteer, Bob Harkins, in his light yellow shirt and his slouch sun and fishing hat with his name tag on the front, approaches two older ladies and gives them folders/brochures. He carefully explains the layout of the Wall and talks about some of the people whose names appear on it.

4:30 P.M. Overheard among a group of thirtysomethings:

Line 5, see it?
He used to pitch baseball.
Remember Sallie? He was her first husband.
Didn't he live by the swimming pool?
There were four or five of them.
You mean McCormick's on here, too?
When I went in in '68, that man was dead.

4:45 P.M. A boy asks, "Dad, who fought the war?" No answer. "Dad, who did they fight?"

His brother says derisively, "The enemy, dummy."

5:00 P.M. Captains Duncan B. McIntyre and John D. Benien have each been left a small bouquet of carnations by a man in a cowboy hat, vest and glasses. The man had rushed to a spot on the Wall below the names, carefully unwrapped each bouquet and laid it down. Then he stood back and cried. "I'm an ex-soldier," he says, not wanting to tell his name. "Vietnam, '68. Never

been here before. There's a lot of 'em.... I was in the rifle platoon—you lose half of 'em in a night. Your luck just runs so long." He pauses, then says quietly, "You can say these flowers were left here by Bill Ford from Shawnee, Oklahoma." Then he turns and leaves.

5:01 P.M. Steve Black, the night ranger, takes over for Mike Lucas, who puts away his ladder and says goodbye. Black will be the only ranger on duty until midnight.

5:06 P.M. An elegant trio, two men and a woman, all in black, are discussing the architectural merits of the Wall. Gesturing toward the Washington Monument, one of the men says, "Compare the monumentality of that, done by a man, to this, done by a woman...."

5:15 P.M. In the late afternoon sun the crowd is increasing. Marlene Batelic, originally from Scotland, says, "I just wanted to feel the spirit of these wonderful men who died."

5:18 P.M. Albertine Taylor of Sacramento, California, is with her daughter and three grandchildren, searching for the name of her cousin, Kenna C. Taylor. During the war she was a nurse for the Air Force on Guam, helping to stabilize soldiers in transit to hospitals stateside. She couldn't remember names, "but there's a chill that goes over me as I walk down here—especially when I look to see if I recognize any name. I may not remember names, but I do remember seeing boys coming back with arms or legs gone—or head injuries. Boy, but it was somethin'. I know how these guys suffered. Some still do. I bought a shirt out there on the street. My daughter said, 'Who are you buying that shirt for, Mom?' 'I don't know. I'm just buying it to help one guy, maybe one whose wounds were not on the outside where you can see 'em.'"

5:20 P.M. A French teen walks by and asks her mother what the point of the Wall is. "It's so you remember," says her mother.

Chris Kelley Clark of McKeesport, Pennsylvania, says that the name she touched, Joe T. Shumpert, was that of her uncle. "I was quite young. He was one of the best-looking men I had ever seen. I had a crush on him. He was probably killed when he was in his mid-twenties. He was with the Army." She begins to weep. "This Wall affects me more than I thought it would. Just to see so many names makes it more real, to see how many families were affected—how many suffered grief and loss. I never really felt personally touched by it 'til now."

"It gives me a feeling that I know all the individuals

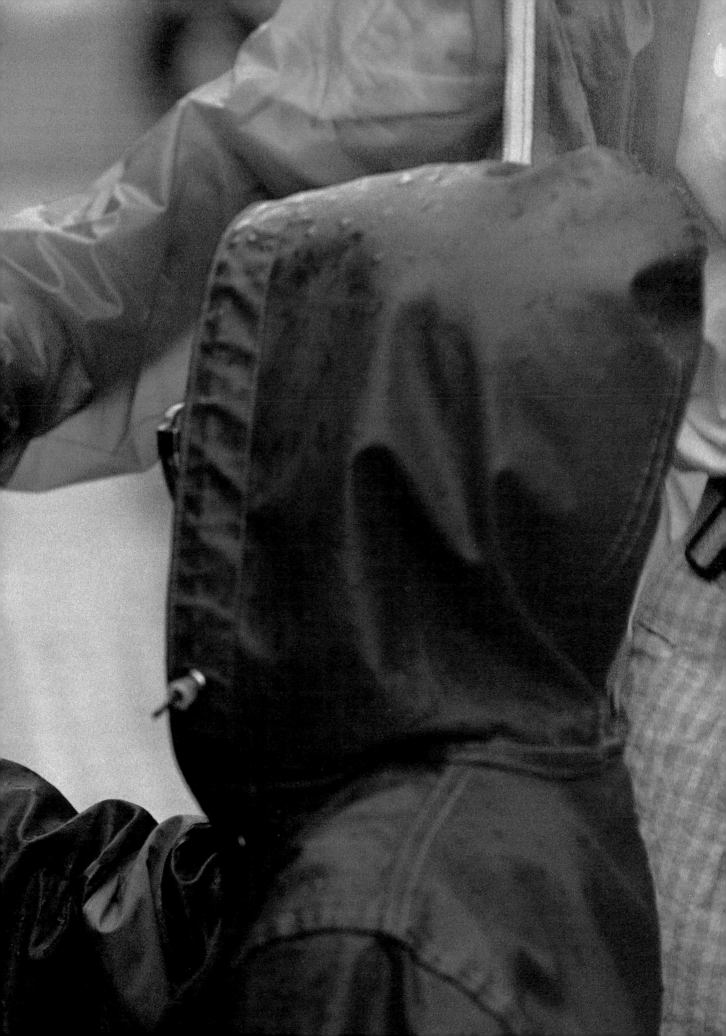

here," says Barry Heffner, explaining why he has visited the Wall a half-dozen times. Heffner was in Vietnam from June of 1967 to July of 1968. "All my Marine Corps buddies get the feeling of knowing everyone on the Wall. It's odd.... I wouldn't make a trip to D.C. without coming here. This is my war, my history. Not the history of Washington or Jefferson or Lincoln that you see in monuments all around here. This one's mine. And they're my buddies."

Volunteer Bob Harkins works with the Simpson family of Tucson, Arizona. They are looking for Ed Simpson's sister's fiance, Dale M. McCauly, a Marine. "There's no way I thought there were this many names here," Ed says. "At the time, we lived in Ohio. I was the last person in town to talk to Dale. He was in 'Nam for just a month before he was hit by a sniper. He came from Uhrichsville, Ohio. They named a street after him in his hometown. McCauly Drive."

5:30 P.M. "After Vietnam I spent eighteen months in Washington," says Leo Fitzgerald, a veteran. "This is my first time back. I'm okay. Walking over from the statue, I was getting worked up. But I'm okay." He nods firmly, reassuringly, holding himself together.

He's one of the brave ones. Frank Bosch, a Wall volunteer and veteran of World War II, Korea and Vietnam, says he had to be dragged to the Wall by his wife the first time. It's hard for everyone, he says. "One family came down, but the man stayed in the car. It happens all the time. They'll get close. But they won't come down. You've got to break that barrier. You've got to face it."

5:32 P.M. Bob Harkins walks over to a family making a rubbing on a crinkled piece of eight-by-ten paper and gives them a narrow piece of Vietnam Veterans Memorial rubbing paper. Someone else needs help. He takes his pointer out to count the names on a high line and then asks a tall man standing nearby if he would help a lady take a name off the Wall.

"It's rewarding to work here," he says. "Many times you talk to people, and they're war casualties. But what people don't know, too, is that on this Wall there are twenty-two different nationalities, boys who didn't have to fight and who died."

Harkins has seen the full range of visitors: the woman who comes over and touches the Wall and says they were going to be married; the survivors—the man who stayed behind when his friend went out and who now comes and pounds on the black slab saying, "It should have been me, it should have been me on the Wall, Eddie, Eddie..."; the Vietnamese, who are bitter that a million of their countrymen died and they're still digging for bodies; the mother who comes to see her son's name and sees also the names of the friends he mentioned in his letters home, right next to his, meaning that they all died the same day, in the same blast; the teenager who comes and sits in front of a certain portion of the Wall for hours—his father. "These are the things that happen every day," says Harkins.

6:00 P.M. A man is crying, leaning against the Wall, his face in his hands. His wife stands beside him, comforting him. Ralph Knerem, 48, from Maple Heights, Ohio, was an Army sergeant with the 173rd Airborne for two combat tours between 1967 and 1969. Though he says he is better now after intensive counseling and since becoming, with his wife, a born-again Christian, he has suffered from severe PTSD ever since his return.

Knerem carries a list of 10 names he wants to see on the Wall, scrawled on a yellow legal pad. The first is his sergeant, on panel 32W.

"My platoon sergeant is up there," he says. "He was killed in '68." Ralph stops talking, overcome with grief. "We were in a special unit that went behind enemy lines. This one time we were captured by the NVA [North Vietnamese Army]. They put a gun up to his head and blew his brains out. Just like that. For no reason.... I relive this thing in my nightmares all the time. I can't turn it off. I feel so much anger at the NVA, and at the bastards in Washington. They taught us to kill, and now what can we do? They ruined my life for twenty-one years. God, I can't stop remembering." He sobs again, looking devastated. "He was my sergeant, a man I looked up to more than anyone. I'm here to put this guy to rest. He was a good man, never cussed. He helped me out so many times. I owe him my life. I've tried to come here before to thank him. It's so damn hard to face the Wall. I came here once, and got as far as the statue, but I couldn't come down to the Wall. I wasn't ready. But this time, I'm here. I need to walk away from this Wall at peace. It's been twenty-one years. I pray this will heal me and end the turmoil in my life."

Later, Ralph leaves an American flag propped against panel 32W, with a note attached:

Dear Sergeant Anderson:
I'm sorry what happened to you in the Nam. It was good being with you, you were top sergeant to me. I know one day I'll see you again.

Yours Truly,
Sergeant Ralph E. Knerem

6:05 P.M. The sun is behind the Lincoln Memorial. People are posing for pictures at the Wall. A little girl is carefully reading the letters in the name "Thomas." "Help me," she tells her slightly older brother. Her father, Mike Powers, remarks, "The Wall is impressive, but what a waste. It was all politics. There better be a heaven, because these guys deserve to be there. It's a national disgrace as well as a national monument."

6:50 P.M. Rita Forward and Melba Ozenne are counting rows. They find Leroy Spiller III, a high school friend. "It's incredible that so many died," says Melba. "I had no idea of the magnitude before seeing this. This is a lot of lives, and then you think of all the families affected by it."

6:58 P.M. Bob Harkins is at the ranger kiosk, punching up variations on name spellings on the computer, handing out maps, suggesting other monuments to visit and free band concerts to attend in and around D.C..

Harkins was with the Park Service before the Wall went up. And within a year of the Wall being built, he became a volunteer. "At that time, the Wall belonged to no one," he recalls. "The government didn't accept it until 1984—so there was a two-year period when the volunteers 'owned' the Wall.... We've lost a lot of them—either they reach a burn-out stage or feel they have other things they want to do with their lives. But many of the guys enjoy being down here, meeting the public; and they have a good disposition for it. It seems to be tough to get volunteers from the Vietnam era. I guess they are surrounded by too many ghosts."

7:00 P.M. Three children play tag at the Wall. "You're It!" one shouts, and the game moves from the pathway to the lawn. Oddly, their gaiety does not seem out of place.

7:10 P.M. In the early evening shadows the Wall is getting dark. People still count, point, take pictures, put their fingers on the Wall. It's the same ritual, the same surprise at finding a name, the same quick sorrow at finding death.

Bill Dean has been walking along the Wall for a long time. Moving from one place to another. He isn't crying, he doesn't have children in tow, he doesn't touch the Wall. He doesn't seem moved, but he's been here a long time.

On a business trip from Corvallis, Oregon, for Hewlett Packard, Dean made his boss promise to drag him to the Wall if he didn't go himself. "I felt pretty good until I walked down in," he says. Dean was in Vietnam in 1968

and 1969. "It wasn't until they built the Wall ten years ago that I felt that we were given recognition. But I've never been able to drag myself here. I've flown into D.C. on business, and I've been to Dulles with two hours between flights. This is the first time I've made it. I was fine until I walked over here.

"It's interesting how it sneaks up on you, because it's so subtle and so fragile and all of a sudden you feel like you're in deep and that's the same sort of thing that happened in Vietnam. We kind of gradually got into it, and all of a sudden we were in it so deep that we really couldn't get out.

"I belong to the Vietnam Helicopter Pilots Association, and I've been trying to find details about people who were shot down and I can't remember a lot of names, it's like there's a blank. Eventually, I'll figure it out.... There was a pilot that I distinctly remember. He was on his last thirty days and he had stopped flying. His replacement came in. I don't remember his name, but everybody called him Pop A Top. He'd always hang out when we were having a little beer bust and he'd pop beers for people and he got this name, Pop A Top. So he went on one last mission—I remember the guy had a wife, several kids. He was going home, he was thrilled about it, and he went out on one last mission and the rotors failed. I watched him go down.

"Vietnam wasn't just a combat zone. There was a lot of camaraderie. There was a lot of brotherhood. There isn't one person on this Wall that didn't have several dozen brothers over there. People you'd never seen, never would have met, and you're brought close together. That was something that was very significant about Vietnam.... You could probably pick any name on the Wall and go around and find people who were closer to that individual than to anybody you'll ever find anywhere in any relationship. One good friend of mine who's been flying for the Coast Guard for the past few years lost his entire wedding party in one day. The guys who had been in the wedding party were in his unit and were all killed at the same time. I'm trying to get him to come out of his shell a little bit and talk about it, get it off his chest. For him it's like, All of the people that are close to me are gone. Why should I even care?

"When I got home from the war, I didn't say anything about Vietnam to my parents or anybody else. Vietnam was something I put behind me. You might find this hard to believe. There were a lot of times I woke up in the night and I couldn't fathom whether I had really gone to Vietnam, experienced these things or whether I was dreaming them. Once the Wall was under way, I began to dig. I started going through boxes, I started

pulling out photographs. I tried to document the whole time I was there.

"After opening that up, I opened up. I had some significant things that were bothering me that I could not get out of my system and finally began to talk about them to people close to me. Now I feel like I'm doing pretty good."

7:30 P.M. Garrett Chesnutt, an airline pilot on layover, came to find his father's name. Chesnutt is 33, handsome, brown-haired, animated, not visibly sad or troubled. At panel 2E, he counts rows and then spots it: Chambless M. Chesnutt. An Air Force fighter pilot, Chambless was shot down in 1965, when Garrett, one of three children, was seven. "I don't remember him as a person," he says. "When I see his name, I only see pictures of him." He remembers that when his father was killed, his mother held the family together. "She talked quite a bit about Dad. They'd been married nine or ten years when he was killed." She married again, to another fighter pilot, but she won't come to the Wall. "She has a tough time with this," he says.

"I felt cheated," says Garrett, "and I feel cheated now. I went through an angry period. It would have been nice to have a dad growing up. Everybody else I knew had one. When I look at my seven-year-old son, I think about how if I were killed, he wouldn't know me, and that hurts."

6. QUIET NIGHT

8:00 P.M. A father and his nine-year-old son are looking at the name of a friend the man knew in high school. "I think it's real sad," says the boy. His dad tells him how his buddy used to like fixing cars. "He was real good with cars. It was a waste to see him die." To his son: "They did so much for the country, and it took so long to pay them back with this Wall.... They went over there modestly, and they wanted to do their job and come back, and some didn't, and I think this is how they would want to be remembered. And over there is Mr. Lincoln. He also had a hard time, and had his life cut short. I think these boys are in good company with him. It's breathtaking how the Wall comes out of the ground, sweeps up, and then disappears, just like the lives of these boys."

8:15 P.M. The sun is setting, but there are at least 70 visitors at the Wall, clusters of people moving from one place to another.

8:30 P.M. Bill Dean, the man from Oregon, is still at the Wall.

8:45 P.M. A tour group of elderly women from Wisconsin leaves the Wall to where the buses are parked, moving fast. Says one of them, "I've seen it before. I liked it better in the day."

8:48 P.M. Wayne Lopresti from Stockertown, Pennsylvania, his wife and two young children, a boy and a girl, have a computer printout from the kiosk. The mother arranges the children to point at a name on the Wall—Ray Hawk—and she stands back and takes a photograph. Wayne walks back, tears in his eyes. "I have three of 'em," he says, looking down at the names on his piece of paper. "I didn't know him. My wife knew him. I didn't know any of them, but I served at that time—I was in the Navy—and the way I look at it is these are all my brothers."

9:00 P.M. It's dark around the Wall—a remarkable contrast to the magnificently lighted Lincoln nearby—cooler, quieter than the afternoon, but still bustling. Bunches of people create a carnival atmosphere around the vendors' stalls, the Lincoln Memorial, the soldier's statue. Knots of people still peer over the directories at both ends of the Wall. Many kids, many strollers. "Let's go boys!" says one man to his children. "See if we can find him..." His voice trails off as he tries to keep up his spirits.

There's an occasional siren in the distance, the hum of crickets and the murmur of voices. As the procession into the gash continues, the dim spotlights at the base of every other panel throw cartoonish shadows against the black granite.

9:06 P.M. "This was a friend of mine and your dad," says a woman to her young boys. "He died in Vietnam."

Two young men, one in a batik shirt, one in plaid shorts, trace the name of William Carter. Chad Thoreau, an architecture student at Notre Dame, wears an MIA bracelet with Carter's name engraved. He bought the bracelet four years ago, through a ROTC program. "It's kind of just an understanding of what happened," Chad says. "A show of support, I guess. It's something I feel like I should do. Something I want to do.... I guess it's just my small attempt to say, 'I have one person, out of all these people, on my wrist.' The thing goes on forever."

Chad's friend Chris Burke, a grad student at Georgetown, says his father was in Vietnam as a doctor. "He wasn't really in the thick of it," he says. "And he doesn't really talk about it." A friend from the war came to visit once, and that was the first time Chris heard his father talk about the war. "It's scary," he says. "I mean, each one of these was an individual who had a family, who really felt a huge loss when they died. It really personalizes the war, even though I was only four when it ended. I was just here a couple of days ago, and you know how people leave things. I read a poem written by somebody who apparently lost a couple friends. And he wrote about that day. It was really sad."

9:20 P.M. "We kill this many people in car accidents every year, and we don't think anything of it," says a man to his companions.

9:25 P.M. A noisy tour passes by. Mostly children, walking fast. "I could have sworn the Egyptians built this," says one.

9:27 P.M. A young couple stands near the eastern wing, making a rubbing. "We just got married," says the man, "and we're getting last names from each person in our family. Like, my mother was a Hardison and my father was a Case. And we've got the Case. And her mother was a Musgrove, and her dad was a Wilcox, and we've got a Wilcox and a Musgrove...."

"Something to remember," says the new bride.

9:34 P.M. Someone has left a beret with a dog tag pinned to it at panel 6E. With it is a picture and a name: Robinson, Harry. His name is not in the directory; he may be a survivor, one of those left behind.

9:45 P.M. Jim Kolbe, a Vietnam veteran and a member of Congress from Arizona, has brought a new office intern to the Wall. The congressman, who helped pass legislation to build the Wall, visits at least ten times a year, he says. "I always come at night, usually around eleven or twelve."

9:55 P.M. "It's taller than Daddy," says a little boy. "It's taller than two daddies," says his brother.

9:56 P.M. "I was a Presbyterian minister in Connecticut during the War," says Dr. George Pera, who now ministers in Alexandria, Virginia. He comes frequently, always at night. "There's something sacred here at night." Tonight Pera is escorting three women around the memorial. "I buried four guys here," he tells them. "I buried Philip Benn six months after I married him." Pera is a jovial man with a hearty voice. But his demeanor changes as he speaks. "Another time I went with a military officer to a father with the cremated remains of his son. He was a six-foot tall boy in a six-inch box." Pera chokes up. He's crying. "I still break up when I see the Wall," he explains. "It breaks my heart. Every one of these names is a human being with a family and it goes on forever.... They're all so young."

10:00 P.M. Peter Slack is visiting the Wall with his young daughter Stephanie, who thinks the place at this time of night "scary." Her father, a geography teacher in Fort Lauderdale, Florida, went to Vietnam in 1990, traveling from Saigon to Hanoi. "They have a couple of museums that they call war museums," he says. "It's their side of the story, something I had never heard before. But the average person on the street is glad to see us. In Saigon one guy said, 'You're American. We haven't seen you here in fifteen years.'

"I think the Wall is awesome, perfect. It's part of the earth, for one thing, and the sheer size of it pretty much says it all about the war, the number of lives lost. And this doesn't account for the millions of Vietnamese. You add those up together and multiply the total by at least three for each family that was affected by somebody's death or injury, and you've got millions of people who were affected by the war. It wasn't at all worth it."

"We should never have gone. Way back in '46 Ho Chi Minh wanted to declare his country independent, and he actually quoted from the U.S. Constitution. At first we were on his side because he helped us fight the Japanese, but instead of sticking by him, we stabbed him in the back. Had we stayed with him, it would have been a different world. All these people definitely wouldn't be up here. If we had just walked away after the French lost, everything would be the same except all these people would still be alive. At least they wouldn't have died that way."

10:02 P.M. A lady from Texas: "One of the most moving memorials out here. Once you see the names like this, it's incredible the number of people who died in that war."

10:05 P.M. A man by the east directory is looking up the father of a woman he works with. "She asked me to make a rubbing of his name if I got up here," he says. "Her father died when she was two or three years old, so she never really knew him."

10:30 P.M. At the kiosk someone asks for a printout for "Q-u-a-c-r-o-n-e."

At the Wall, a man exclaims, "Do you know how many walls it would take to list all the Vietnamese killed? Sixty. Sixty of these walls."

10:50 P.M. Still they keep coming. No more babies, but children still. They peer at the *The Three Servicemen* statue. They look in the books, keep walking by the Wall. It feels like it could keep up all night.

11:03 P.M. Crickets chirp as traffic lights click from red to green to yellow on a deserted Constitution Avenue. The air has cooled. Only a few people walk the Wall, moving like figures in a candled cave, dark shapes with fuzzy edges thrown against black stone. Ghosts.

11:10 P.M. Several participants from a Japanese-American student conference have ventured out to see the Wall. One, a woman who speaks English, considers the Wall "too heavy and dark. Too obvious. In Japan we might not want to have our family's name out there in a public place where everyone can see it, touch it, and where rain falls on it. The Japanese don't go to public monuments to pay homage to soldiers. It is too obvious,

too public. We are more private."

11:25 P.M. A heavy man in a light, long-sleeved shirt is putting both hands on the Wall, staring at a name. He remains motionless. Finally, he's able to speak. "I've been trying to face this Wall since they put it here. I've come from Texas and this is my third or fourth run at it.

He starts crying, talking about his friend on the Wall between sobs. "He was like a brother. They butchered him." The man looks heartbreakingly desolate. "I've wrestled with it a lot of years. I've got to put it to bed," he says as he walks off crying.

11:30 P.M. Sprinklers come on to water the lush grass, creating a misty halo above the Wall. Some of sprinklers are not lined up right and water sprays over the Wall, onto the walkway. Some of the spotlights begin to smoke; one pops out.

11:31 P.M. In the dark, a man comments, "It's handsome in its simplicity." He notes that many of the original designs for the Washington Monument—now a simple, brightly lighted obelisk reflected in the Wall—were very ornate.

Toby Whitney, a student of Comparative Literature, is home from a year in Paris. He is often drawn to the memorial, especially after hours. "It was a dark period of our history," he explains. "So most Washingtonians will tell you to come here at night when it's peaceful. There's less traffic, less noise. It's more genuine.

"I think it's the best modern monument in the world. A modern monument, never done before. There are other ways of expressing the idea, but aside from the Soviet monument for World War II, there are none in France, Spain, Germany that people enjoy as much as this. It's not Greek, not classical, it's American. It uses light, it uses modern technology, and there is a point to touching it."

MIDNIGHT Park ranger David Krewson closes the kiosk. Only a few people wander along the path by the Wall as park ranger Black collects mementos at the end of his shift. He picks up Ralph Knerem's flag and note (artifact 8/76), four more letters, a flag with an MIA-POW bracelet attached, and the black beret with Harry Robinson's dog tags.

It's quiet enough to hear the loose pavers of the walkway clunk under people's feet.

7. THE LONG VIGIL

12:35 A.M. The Wall looks like water one moment, like a dock edged with candles the next. It is deserted except for a man sitting on a nearby bench. He wears a blue baseball cap with the Marine insignia pinned on. Ed Hultberg, from Blairstown, New Jersey, is in Washington to attend a reunion of the First Marine Division. He was in Vietnam from May of 1966 to November of 1967.

He drives to Washington four or five times a year just to visit the Wall, often at night. "It's the time for reflection. Just to sit here, pay my respects to my brothers, my former brothers. You know, just reflect on everything. It's an amazing place. Up until two years ago I sort of ignored the whole Vietnam experience, to the point where I just made sure people who were my friends *weren't* there. And, I don't know, just all of a sudden I started getting real melancholy about it. I was struggling, doing a lot of crying and everything. And somebody told me to visit this place, that it would help out. And I did, and it's just an amazing place. I can't believe how much it's helped out."

Sometimes Hultberg puts on the volunteer's yellow cap, one of the few vets who can do it. "I still find it a little intense," he says. "Like, I was here for Veterans Day last year, and I don't think I made it fifty feet down that marble there and it just became too intense for me. I had to turn back." He lights up a cigarette.

"I have a few friends on the Wall," he continues. "A guy I went to boot camp with, a friend who was from Pennsylvania. And this is the place where I met the son of a Navy pilot at two o'clock in the morning. It was down at 1975, right in the middle of the Wall, and this young, nice-looking man ran down. He was in a jogging outfit. And he stopped right there. And he sat down Indian-style right on the pavers there, and just sat in front of that panel. After he walked over to the soldiers statue I just asked him: 'You know somebody on the wall?' And the guy opened up right away. It was like he was waiting to talk, and he just poured all this stuff out about his father's death. It was quite an experience.

"But you know, I look down at this Wall, and I see, oh, you know, fifty-eight thousand, one hundred and eighty-three names on that Wall, and it just seems like a terrible waste of life. Nothing was really accomplished.

"I've been here as late as four o'clock in the morning. I could not pull myself away from this place. I couldn't. The first two times I came down here I had planned to come down for three days and wound up staying five. The second time I made up car trouble and said I couldn't get back. I just could not tear myself away from here.

"I think the war robbed me of a lot of happiness. I really do. I think for years I was real withdrawn and unhappy. I think I was bitter, I think I still am a little bit. Rather than teaching me responsibility, I think it wasted a lot of that. I have a failed marriage. I read that the divorce rate among Vietnam vets is something like in the ninetieth percentile. And the average income for a Vietnam vet is like $7,000 a year. And what really shook me up is that almost three times as many men have committed suicide as died in the war. We're talking 130,000 men committing suicide."

[Mortality rates among Vietnam veterans, especially from motor vehicle accidents and "accidental poisonings" (i.e., drug overdoses), have run as much as 17 percent higher than those of the general population. But the high suicide figures—the one recalled by Hultberg was published in a veterans manual in 1980—though widely reported, have been questioned by recent studies. One from the Centers for Disease Control states that approximately 9,000 Vietnam veterans have committed suicide since the war ended.]

Every now and then someone strolls by. Hultberg continues: "A lot of my friends who weren't in Vietnam say, 'Get on with your life, Vietnam was twenty-five years ago.' There's one important thing that none of them know: that we have to keep their memory alive. Those guys down there on that Wall. It's our job to keep them alive."

3:45 A.M. Ed Hultberg leaves the Wall.

4:00 A.M. Ranger Krewson does a quick sweep of the Wall to see what was left since he came on duty. Only a flag and a comb. He puts the mementos in marked plastic sacks and logs them at the ranger kiosk.

5:00 A.M. Krewson goes home. Crickets chirp. There are no visitors at the Wall, which seems to float in the darkness, a luminous black line on a field of black. It is the first time all night that there has been no visitor to the Wall.

5:10 A.M. The sky is light around the edges of the horizon behind the Washington Monument. Three people in work clothes pass by the Wall, heads turned toward the names.

5:40 A.M. The lights at the base of the Wall continue to glow even after daylight is well established. A jogger pauses at the soldiers statue, turning back to look at the Wall before trotting on through the grove of trees at the south edge of the memorial.

6:00 A.M. The lights at the Wall click off.

6:25 A.M. More joggers. Harry Abrams, in shorts, runs slowly past the Wall, looking at the names. He is a hospital administrator for the Department of Veterans Affairs in St. Petersburg, Florida. "I always run by here when I come to Washington," he says. "I feel like these guys deserve our attention, they were ignored so long."

6:45 A.M. Three men and a woman arrive with a rubber hose, rubber buckets, soapy water and long-handled scrub brushes. Volunteers from nearby Bolling Air Force Base wash the Wall once a week, says Chris Knight, an Air Force technician, "to remove the fingerprints, the lipstick marks (from kissing the names) and any other spills. Even though people are asked not to carry drinks along the Wall, there once was an emergency call to us because someone spilled Coke all over a panel. And Coke is acid at base."

Dan Miller, 29, also a technician, says that none of the volunteers are Vietnam vets. "I'm doing this because we gotta remember these guys," he says. "We finally got a monument to them. I know they deserve a lot more than they got when they came home."

Robert and Lorraine Aida, husband and wife volunteers, are slathering on soap from their buckets. "It's the only living monument in the world," says Lorraine.

For the next hour, the volunteers work methodically to clean each panel.

7:00 A.M. Four big men, one in a wheelchair, move slowly down the walkway toward the fold. Wearing caps and jackets decorated with military insignias, all of them are members of the First Marine Division, in town for a reunion.

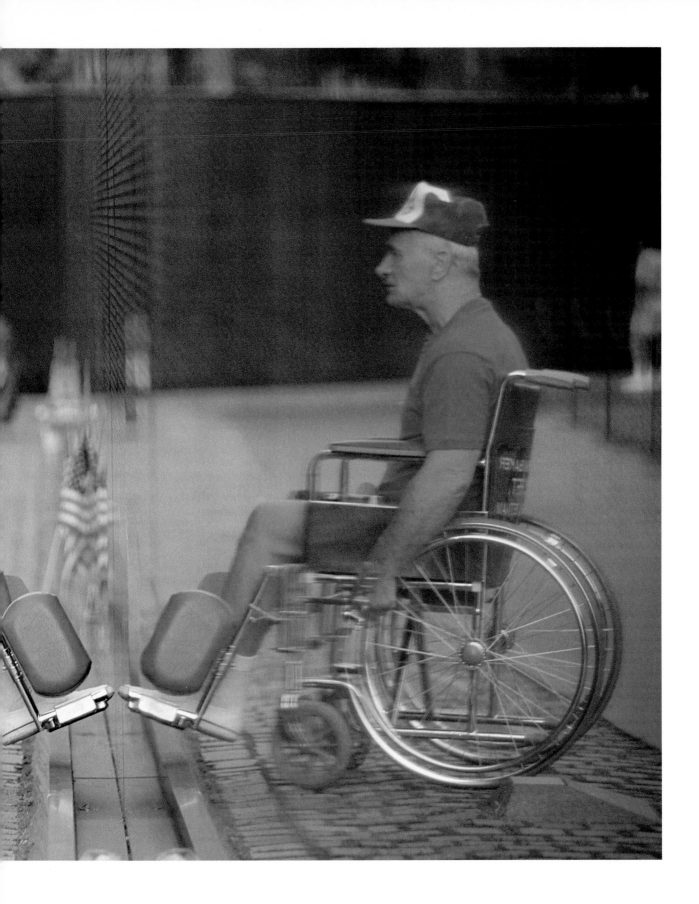

Lawrence Pennybaker, on wheels, is a veteran of three wars. "He's just looking for a few of his friends," says one of the men with him. But the former master sergeant is uncomfortable about being here. The last time he'd come, four years ago, he'd gone in the black of night because he didn't want anyone to see him break down. "I'm really ashamed my name isn't on the wall," Pennybaker says. Silence. And he pushes his chair toward another name. He won't tell how he lost his leg. "It wasn't in war," he says bluntly.

In Vietnam for two tours, Pennybaker, now 69, was known as Pop. He left Vietnam as a master sergeant.

"I didn't mind visiting the Iwo Jima monument," he says. "That makes me proud. The Vietnam Wall makes me sick, because of the waste in that war.

"World War II was a good fight. Korea, too. You could at least see the enemy. But Vietnam was a hellhole. A lot of these guys died for no good reason. Look at 'em up there. There's that kid, Hicks, and Lyle Morris—there's so many of them." He pauses to stare at the Wall, the memories bringing tears to his eyes. "This is crazy," he says, "I shouldn't have come here. I'll never come again. It's just a crazy, mixed-up world. Most of these guys were eighteen and nineteen years old.... Those were my boys. They would follow me through hell. Hicks, Morris—Morris was a sergeant, mean and tough, a go-getter Marine. He was twenty-one or twenty-two years old when he was hit by an RPG [rocket-propelled grenade]. What a waste, what a waste."

8:00 A.M. The light is full now. Mike Lucas swings open the windows of the ranger kiosk as the first tour bus pulls up to the curb. Another day begins at the Vietnam Veterans Memorial—the Wall to heal a nation.

FREDERICK O JONES • LARRY W CHAN
CARL W THOMPSON • PAUL R CARSON • GERAL
RUDOLPH C VALENTA • DANIEL R HOFFM
CHESTER A LUC • ELDON L SHARLEY • FRANKLI
WILLIAM J JIMENEZ ACEVEDO • AUDLEY D
RONALD K SCHULZ • IRVING J BR
LLEN C SCURLOCK • JOHN C HAYES • LARRY J MILL
BARRY LEE BROWN • WALLACE J DEPREO • LA
PAUL A STOKES • ROBERT M WEB
RICHARD H DEER • WESLEY S SMELTON
ALVIN B CHILDRESS • FLOYD W FRAZIER Jr • ROBE
EDWARD J DOGGETT • RICHARD J PRIVITAR
JAMES M HINKLE • WILLIAM J M
HARRY H BLACK Jr • PAT C BRANNON
ANTON J JOHN OBRIEN • RANDALL E MAGGO
WILLIAM R LEWIS Jr • ROBERT H CLIFTON
LIFFORD A HOSTEN • HARRY D McWHINN
RUFUS R FALKNER Jr • SANFORD I FINGER • T
LEONARD O MAQUILING • ROBERT A NICKOL
SAMUEL A AMEY • BRENT P CLEVELAND
MES L VAUGHAN • BOBBY B WHITE • JOHN P CARF
JERRY E TEW • VICTOR D WILLIAMS • KENNET
JACK A CARNES • DARRELL HOGAN
DAVID O SMITHWICK • DONALD C TALLMAN
ANGEL ALARID QUEVEDO • CARL D TOMLIN
ROBERT F QUANDT • JACK L DECAIR
JERRY C THOMAS • DENNIS I DA
ARLIE R MANGUS • JERRY D MA

...MAS H ... ROBERT O GOODMAN ... DA...

NEY A COTTRELL • GARY L MIZNER • JEFFREY R STOK...
LONE • ADDISON W PAGE Jr • RAFAEL PEREZ VERD...
SEPH M FEENEY • DAVID J EUNES • DENNIS R HINTO...
O SILOS • THOMAS J STANUSH • MICHAEL L DARRA...
OHN S CHIRIN • HUGO A GAYTAN • RICKY ALAN PA...
CARLS MERLINO • EDDIE B HUBBINS • RALPH N L...
B SEARING • HARRY O BOWLES • BARRY A BOWMA...
EVERETT • DAVID R HOUSER • ALVIS T BARRINGTON
ERT J BARTON • PATRICK J BRESLIN • JOHN H BROW...
ARIENS • ALAN R BOONE • WILLIAM E WHITEMAN
OWN • MARSHALL W WILLIAMS • BILLIE LEE COLEMA...
M A SHELTON • HERMAN C CAHOON • PAUL R FOL...
J • LARRY J PORTER • DANIEL S SALAS • ROY D BARN...
Y A COWAN • DANIEL O DYE • MAURICE E GARRETT
NY J MENSEN • BILLY J MORRIS • NICK N RODRIGU...
FRISBIE • LONNIE W MITCHELL • ANTHONY P QUI...
YOSHIDA • BRUCE A ABDULLAH • MICKEY B EVELAN...
REEN • EDWARD L HIMES • MICHAEL L AUTZENHEIS...
O SKINNER • STANLEY W TAYLOR • ALBERT R TRUDE...
JACKSON • DONALD F VAUGHAN • JAMES C WAY...
Y L HAYNES • JIM C O'RILEY • GENE W STOCKM...
LINGER • HARDY A CLEVELAND • MICHAEL M FAR...
ROBLES MARTINEZ • ROBERT E RYAN • JAMES M SE...
B WARD Jr • STEPHEN J HUSKEY • CLIFFE S JOHNS...
AS P FRANK • MICHAEL L HINO • JOSE M MALDONA...
L KENDALL • ERROL KENT • ERNEST J MONTELEON...
RD C DORITY • DAVID L GINN • HARVEY D JOHNS...
VIN A NORRIS • JAMES R PANTALL • JERRY LEE V...

CONTRIBUTORS

This book would not have been possible without the excellent work—and generous spirit—of the reporters and photographers who contributed their talents to it.

REPORTERS

Naomi Cutner Freelance journalist Cutner is a former LIFE staff reporter and current contributor. She has been a writer at the United Nations, a book editor and was chief researcher on "Childhood in America," a public television program about children at risk. A student at the University of California, Berkeley, during the late 1960's and early 1970's, Cutner marched against the war. Her day at the Wall brought to mind "a friendly boy named Dave from my high school class in Los Angeles who was killed in Vietnam. It's sad to think back to the carefree summer days when my friends and I flirted and laughed with him on the beach."

David Ewing Duncan Author of two books, *From Cape to Cairo: An African Odyssey* and *Pedaling The Ends of The Earth*, of articles in magazines such as *The Atlantic* and *Harper's,* as well as commentary for National Public Radio, Duncan says he "grew up watching Walter Cronkite on television deliver the daily casualty count from Vietnam." Now finishing a biography of Spanish explorer Hernando de Soto, Duncan lives in Baltimore with his wife and two young children.

Janet Mason An assistant editor of LIFE, Mason has been with the magazine since 1961. Among the hundreds of stories she has reported was a major piece about Vietnam veterans recovering from heroin addiction in a VA hospital in California. "The day at the Wall," she says, "was a reprise of tales I heard twenty-five years earlier—told today from a perspective of survival and distant memory."

Sue Allison Massimiano "The first time I went to the Wall, I couldn't look at it," says writer Massimiano. "My brother had died, not in the war, but like these boys, tragically, and too soon." A reporter for LIFE for eight years, Massimiano is now a freelance writer and still frequent contributor to LIFE. She is also the author, with photographer Alen MacWeeney, of *Bloomsbury Reflections* and currently lives with her husband in Washington, D.C.

Sasha Nyary LIFE staff reporter Nyary has worked on many stories since joining the magazine in 1989, ranging in scope from the legacy of Martin Luther King to the perils of skin cancer. A political science graduate of Wellesley College in 1988, her earliest memories of the war come from the television news at the family dinner table. "My parents were vehemently opposed to the war," she says. "The strength of their feelings was seminal in leading me to the Quaker faith, which counts nonviolence as a fundamental tenet of its creed."

Steven Petrow A freelance writer and editor, Petrow has contributed to various publications, from the *Los Angeles Times* to LIFE. He has written about Haiti, where he lived for two months, and migrant farm workers on the east coast. He also has written three books about AIDS, the most recent of which is *When Someone You Know Has AIDS: A Practical Guide*. As a teenager Petrow traveled to Washington with his mother to participate in various antiwar protests. "It wasn't until working on this story, however, that I finally realized the distinction between the War and the warrior," he says. Petrow lives in New York City.

Henry Sidel A New York native, freelance researcher and actor Sidel is a 1990 philosophy graduate from Carleton College. During his brief career in the world of journalism he has lent his research skills to such magazines as *Harper's, The New Yorker* and *Vanity Fair,* as well as to LIFE. Sidel was also the assistant editor of LIFE's *More Reflections on the Meaning of Life.*

Stephanie Slewka A former Washington bureau chief for LIFE, Slewka is a freelance writer and television producer based in Washington, D.C. Too young to remember much about the war in Vietnam, she has a vivid recollection of her parents picking up a young Vietnam veteran hitchhiking through Europe after his tour. "He talked and talked about the war and showed off his good luck hat, festooned with grenade pins," says Slewka. "Then he was gone, without his hat. We never found him, but we still have his talisman."

PHOTOGRAPHERS

Bill Eppridge Born in Buenos Aires and raised in Nashville and Richmond, Eppridge began his photography career in 1953 as a "chaser" (e.g., of ambulances) for the Wilmington *Sunday Star*. He began working for LIFE in 1962, shooting everything from race riots in the American south to revolutions in Latin America. As a staff photographer for LIFE until 1972, Eppridge covered many major world events, including four months with the Marines in Vietnam in 1966 and the assassination of Robert Kennedy. His coverage of RFK's campaign and death will be the subject of a Harcourt Brace Jovanovich book to be published in the summer of 1993.

Frank Fournier Born in France, Fournier wanted to go to Vietnam as a photographer in the late 1960's, but his parents convinced him to continue his education in medicine. Four years later he moved to New York to begin his photographic career. Since then Fournier has photographed for every major publication and won numerous awards, including a World Press Photo of the Year prize for his picture of a victim of the Colombian volcano disaster and the World Press Foundation first prize for his pictures of Rumanian children with AIDS. Fournier is a member of Contact Press Images.

Lori Grinker New York native Grinker began her career in photography when her class assignment on young boxers was published in *Inside Sports*. (One of the boxers she met was a 14-year-old named Mike Tyson, whom Grinker has continued to photograph over the years.) Since then she has won numerous awards for work that has appeared in LIFE, the *New York Times Magazine*, *Newsweek* and *People*. A member of Contact Press Images, Grinker is currently working on a photo project about the effects of war on veterans throughout the world.

Charles Harbutt A veteran of the civil rights and anti-war movements, Harbutt photographed the first March on Washington in 1965 for LIFE. Lecturer, professor and a founding member of Archive Pictures Inc., his work has been featured in numerous publications and books, including *America in Crisis*, a photographic documentary of the turbulent '60s. Harbutt lives and works in New York City.

Joe McNally After beginning his journalistic career as a copyboy for the New York *Daily News* in 1976, McNally has spent most of the last two decades photographing for the world's most prestigious publications, including the *New York Times*, *Paris Match*, *Sports Illustrated* and *National Geographic*. Also a frequent contributor to LIFE, McNally has earned a number of prizes, including a Page One Award, for his photojournalism. He lives with his wife and two children just outside of New York City.

Christopher Morris Too young to have covered the Vietnam War, Morris has nevertheless been in most of the world's hotspots since the early 1980's. He has photographed antinuclear demonstrations in Germany, riots in the Philippines, the U.S. invasion of Panama, the guerrilla war in Afghanistan and Operation Desert Storm in the Gulf. A Black Star photographer, last year Morris won both the Robert Capa Gold Medal award from the Overseas Press Club for his coverage of the Yugoslavian civil war and the University of Missouri's prestigious Magazine Photographer of the Year award.

PHOTO CREDITS

Larry Burrows: 9
Bill Eppridge: 15 top, 20, 21, 32, 35, 48, 67, 75, 78-79, 80-81
Frank Fournier: 4, 14 bottom, 26, 30-31, 45 bottom, 51, 52-53, 60-61, 88-89
Lori Grinker: 38, 42, 46-47
Charles Harbutt: 84
Joe McNally: 14 top, 15 bottom, 22, 34, 56-57, 76-77, 82-83, 86-87, 90-91, 92-93
Christopher Morris: front cover, 12-13, 16, 19, 24-25, 27, 28, 36-37, 41, 44-45, 54, 59, 62, 64-65, 66, 68-69, 70, 72-73, endpapers, back cover

ACKNOWLEDGMENTS

Many people helped with this book, but special thanks go to...

The National Park Service and the volunteers of the Vietnam Veterans Memorial. Earl Kittleman, Bill Clarke and Jim Lance of the NPS provided valuable assistance in the early stages of the research. And ranger Mike Lucas and his colleagues at the Wall, as well as "yellow caps" Sid George, Emmelene Gura, Bill Harkins and their incredible helpmates, were invaluable guides throughout the long day. Duery Felton, curator of the NPS's Vietnam Veterans Memorial Collection, provided a rare look into his archives.

Steven Silver and the staff of the Post Traumatic Stress Disorder unit at the Veterans Affairs Coatesville Medical Center. And the men of PTSD Unit 59B at Coatesville, who shared their pain with us.

George Wieser for getting the book off the ground—and to the printer. Tony Meisel for designing it. Tom Dunne of St. Martins Press for believing in it. Jim Bradshaw, a vet, for encouraging it.

Many people at LIFE Magazine helped on this book and need to be thanked. Murray Goldwaser, for saying early, as he always does, "The answer is yes." Jim Gaines and Dan Okrent, for supporting the project. Derrick Wong and Susan Emmer for grinding through numbers and contracts. Suzie Bolotin, for reading the manuscript. Paula Glatzer for her early and consistent cheerleading. June Goldberg for her moral support and careful reading of the manuscript. Alex Smith for trekking to Washington and acting as chief cook and bottle washer even when there was nothing to cook or wash. Ed Barnes—who drove the RV. Melanie deForest, Hilary Angle and Chris Bender, LIFE interns, for the assistance they gave the photographers at the Wall. Bonnie J. Smith, who kept the hotline at the LIFE News Desk open.

And two people at LIFE who deserve special mention for their consistently special work: Barbara Baker Burrows and Janet Mason. Few stories are done without Bobbi—and the story leading to this book is no exception. She chose the photographers for the assignment, helped orchestrate the logistics for The Day, stayed on site to help coordinate the efforts of the photographers and reporters at the Wall, and edited the thousands of pictures taken. All this with, most importantly, her trademark good cheer, a trait which helps make this business worth it. And there's Jan Mason, who knows better than anyone else what a picture story is and how to do it. The consummate pro, Jan not only ran the show at the Wall, but also reported while there, then worked tirelessly, poring over pictures, and reading, checking and rereading this manuscript. Jan and Bobbi are true LIFErs—and godsends.

Finally, thanks to the hundreds of visitors to the Wall on August 4, 1992, who gave their time and their memories.